DOUBLE TAKE
Two sides One story

VOTES FOR WOMEN

BELINDA HOLLYER

Dedicated to the memory of the suffragettes
whose story is told in this book.

This story is based, as much as possible, on primary source material - the words and
pictures of the people that witnessed the events described. Whilst it is not possible to
know the exact thoughts, feelings and motives of all the people involved, the book aims
to give an insight into the experience of the events, based on the available evidence.

Scholastic Children's Books
Commonwealth House, 1–19 New Oxford Street,
London, WC1A 1NU, UK
A division of Scholastic Ltd
London ~ New York ~ Toronto ~ Sydney ~ Auckland
Mexico City ~ New Delhi ~ Hong Kong

Published in the UK by Scholastic Ltd, 2003

ISBN 0 439 97894 7

Printed and bound by Nørhaven Paperback A/S, Denmark

Cover image supplied by Hulton Archive/Getty Images

2 4 6 8 10 9 7 5 3 1

The right of Belinda Hollyer to be identified as the author of this
work has been asserted by her in accordance with the Copyright,
Designs and Patents Act, 1988.

Contents

Prologue

THE WOMAN IS ALONE in her cell, late at night. It is cold in the cell and the air is clammy and damp. It smells of misery – of despair and the loss of hope, of unwashed bodies and spilled urine and worse. The only light is a faint beam through a slot in the door.

The woman is very frightened. She's a fighter; there's no question of her giving up. She knows her protest is right. She will never give up; she would rather die. But she is frightened of what will happen to her next.

She is sick – sick with desperate hunger and thirst, for she has been on a hunger strike for days. She is utterly exhausted, for she has been pacing her cell for 22 hours without pausing. The warders come to peer through the slot in her door, and go away to whisper to each other in disbelief: can she *really* still be on her feet? But she is – just. She knows she may faint again; that she will be at the mercy of the doctors again; that they may not let her out again before she collapses. She is worried about her friends, many of whom are also in prison – also sick, also close to collapse.

But she does not – cannot – *will not* – give up.

The man is alone in his study, late at night. He sits at his desk writing, and a pool of light falls on the piles of papers in front of him. He is catching up on his work while the house is quiet. His beloved children are safe in bed; his fascinating and distracting wife is out at a party.

The man is writing letters to friends, notes for speeches, answers to questions, summaries of arguments. He also makes time to write in his diary, where he records the day's events and the things that matter to him – how other politicians are behaving, how he is trying to get his policies accepted, how he can convince voters to support his party.

He knows about the woman in prison, and about many other women in prisons all around the country. After all, it is his laws that have put them there – he is the Prime Minister. But he seldom mentions the women in his diary. He believes they are hysterical and misguided fools; that what they are asking for is senseless and impossible. He thinks that they have brought their punishments on themselves. If they would only promise to give up their irrational fight, he would arrange for them all to be released.

In the meantime, he ignores their protests as best he can. He has no intention of giving in.

Introduction

IN TWENTY-FIRST CENTURY Britain, almost everyone over the age of 18 has the right to vote in both local and national elections. Only a few adults (such as those in prison) are excluded. In fact, voting is something most people in Britain take for granted. A hundred years ago, however, it was a very different story. In 1900 in Britain, less than one third of all adults were allowed to vote. Decisions made by local councils and in the national parliament at Westminster affected everyone's lives, but most people in the country couldn't do anything to influence those decisions. If they didn't like any of Britain's laws or didn't agree with the men elected to the local council or to the national parliament, they couldn't vote to change them. Only a few people could.

In 1900 the right to vote was restricted in two ways: by your ownership of property, and by your sex. If you were an adult man who owned or occupied property of a certain value, you could register to vote. That meant about 30 per cent of adult men couldn't vote, because they weren't rich enough or didn't live in the right places. But if you were an adult woman you couldn't vote at all, no matter how much property you owned or where you lived. No woman was allowed to register, or to vote, in national elections, and no woman could stand for election as a local council or parliamentary candidate, either.

But British women had not always been excluded from voting. In the Middle Ages, hundreds of years earlier, some women had been accepted as voters. Others had even voted in local elections in the early 1800s – at that time, about 500,000 women were on local electoral registers. Those women had to own a certain amount of property, as did the men who voted at that time.

During the 1800s, however, three important reform laws were passed by the national parliament. These new laws, passed in 1832, 1867 and 1884, in some ways made British elections fairer than they had been. They gave thousands more middle-class and working-class men – and even some agricultural labourers – the right to vote.

But these reform laws specifically excluded all women from voting. That hadn't happened before. The wording of the new laws said that only "male persons" could vote in national elections in Britain. After that, when women tried to register or vote in any local elections most of them were rejected because of those "male persons" words, even though the words were only supposed to apply to parliamentary elections. So as far as the right to vote was concerned, women were worse off after 1867 than they had been in the Middle Ages!

By 1900, though, ideas about British society were slowly beginning to change. Some people believed that women should be able to vote, but the idea of equal rights for women was a new and challenging one. The rules about how people should behave were still very strict, and covered almost every aspect of life.

It is probably hard for us to imagine what this was like. Our twenty-first century society is much more relaxed, and we accept differences and alternatives much more easily. People now generally agree that everyone should be treated equally, no matter what their colour or sex or ethnic origin. But in Britain in 1900 most people would have thought that idea crazy and dangerous. They probably would have believed that it offended against both God's laws and natural laws; even against common sense.

This is the story of Sylvia Pankhurst – one woman who took a stand on women's rights, and whose courage and determination helped to win the vote for every adult woman in Britain. It is also the story of Henry Asquith – a man who opposed votes for women and fought hard against it, but who, in the end, had to admit defeat.

The Sledgehammer
1852 – 1905

HERBERT HENRY ASQUITH was the son of Joseph and Emily Asquith, and was born in Morley on 12 September 1852. When Herbert Asquith was young his brother and sisters called him Bertie, and later on his second wife Margot and the rest of his family called him Henry. But by the time he was a leading Liberal Party politician, and for many years the Prime Minister of Great Britain, most people just called him Asquith. That is the name we use for him in this book.

Joseph Asquith was a Yorkshire woollen merchant – Joseph's own father had owned a cloth mill – and although he was not especially well off he provided a comfortable living for his family. But his sudden death in 1860 left his wife, Emily, and their four young children – William, Herbert Henry, Evelyn and Lilian – in financial difficulties. At first, Emily Asquith's father helped out by sending the two boys to boarding school. Later, when Emily's father also died, her brothers took over responsibility for the Asquith family. Emily Asquith and her two daughters moved to St Leonard's in Sussex, while the two boys were sent off to live with an uncle in London, and to school in the City of London.

It wasn't uncommon then for boys to be sent away to boarding school at an early age, and to spend very little time at home with their families, but Asquith's experience was exceptional. He was effectively orphaned at a very young age and raised by uncles, aunts and schoolmasters, and so he didn't have much of a childhood. His young life must have been sad and difficult for a while because of his father's death and the early separation from his mother. We don't know how Asquith felt about that; but we do know that he struggled with bouts of anxiety and depression throughout his life, so perhaps those early losses affected him profoundly.

Asquith was a clever young man who did very well at school and university. But many of his contemporaries at Oxford University thought he behaved in a superior and cold way – characteristics that masked his shyness. However, despite that shyness, Asquith most certainly had a plan for his life and a set of goals mapped out with care and deliberate calculation. He may have been reserved but he was also a brilliant debater – his style was described as *"cool and courageous and intellectually alert"* and he showed a striking command of language when he spoke in public. In 1874 he became President of the Oxford Union – the University's famous debating society. Even at that early stage, people noticed that he did not try to reconcile his opponents to his point of view – instead, he plunged straight into any argument with no holds barred. No wonder he earned the nickname of *"The Sledgehammer"*!

Asquith wanted a career that made use of his debating skills. The law seemed a good choice and he trained as a lawyer and joined a legal firm in London, but he was not very successful at attracting rich clients. He needed to find a better career, especially because at that time he had a wife and a young family to support.

Asquith decided to enter politics. At that time there were two main political parties in Britain: the Conservative Party and the Liberal Party. Traditionally, Conservative support came from aristocratic land-owning families, while the Liberals attracted rising middle-class professionals. Both parties had achieved important reforms during the nineteenth century, but by the 1880s only the Liberal Party still put parliamentary and economic reforms at the heart of its policies. Asquith's background, education and beliefs made the Liberal Party his natural political home.

In 1886 he stood for election as a Liberal Party candidate for East Fife, in Scotland, and was elected to parliament.

Asquith threw himself enthusiastically into parliamentary life and worked hard to establish himself. He was good-looking, charming and ambitious, and success soon began to come his way. In 1892 the Prime Minister of the day, William Gladstone, gave Asquith the important position of Home Secretary in his new government – so he had already made his mark as an impressive young politician. As Home Secretary, Asquith was responsible for the internal affairs of the country, which included managing the country's security and the police.

Asquith's wife, Helen, died suddenly of typhoid fever in 1891. Asquith had loved her deeply, but when she died he was already in love with another woman as well – the lively and remarkable Margot Tennant. Asquith was determined to marry her, and after three years of his single-minded courtship, Margot finally agreed. They married on 10 May 1894.

Soon after he became Gladstone's Home Secretary, Asquith spoke publicly on the subject that was to make him the declared enemy of thousands of women in Britain: his opposition to women's suffrage. But the Liberal Party lost political power in 1895, and became the opposition instead. Now the Conservative Party was the government.

Asquith didn't enjoy being in opposition. Although he liked political argument he preferred debates to have a practical purpose, he didn't want to argue just for the sake of it. But it was ten years before the Liberal Party won another election, so Asquith had to get used to life away from the focus of political power. He spent a lot of that time travelling the country helping to keep up Liberal Party spirits by making speeches to local associations. In fact, he spent so much time away from parliament that other politicians made jokes about his absence! In the days before television and radio, political meetings in local constituencies were much more important than they are now. Asquith was a popular speaker and when he was advertised, there was always a good turnout to hear him. He became quite famous.

By the summer of 1905 a general election was not far away. Now the Liberal Party was triumphantly riding a wave of popularity, while the Conservatives had lost most of their popular support. Everyone thought that the man who had achieved that turnabout for the Liberals was Asquith. The leader of the Liberal Party was Henry Campbell-Bannerman, and if the Liberals did gain power then he would become Prime Minister. But Asquith was the deputy leader, and he was aiming high.

A Plain Little Woman

1882 – 1905

SYLVIA PANKHURST GREW UP amidst the turmoil of political campaigns and crusades that included all the radical issues of the day. She was the second daughter of Emmeline and Richard Pankhurst, and was born in Old Trafford, in Manchester, on 5 May 1882. Her father, Richard, was a lawyer and a radical thinker who actively supported women's rights, and helped form the Manchester Society for Women's Rights in 1866.

Richard Pankhurst also stood for parliament as a candidate for a new party: the Independent Labour Party. This was formed by a group of trade unionists in 1893, and later developed into the Labour Party. Its key founder and leader was a Scottish trade union leader called James Keir Hardie. Richard Pankhurst was not elected, but he and Keir Hardie remained close colleagues and friends.

As a young girl, Sylvia often accompanied her father when he was campaigning for the Independent Labour Party. As she watched him standing on a soapbox or a chair and arguing the cause of ordinary people with passionate earnestness, Sylvia was moved both to great admiration for her father, and deep compassion for working people. In her mind she compared *"those endless rows of smoke-begrimed little houses with never a tree or a flower in sight"* with her own comfortable home and its two May trees in a big garden.

I would ask myself if it could be just that I should live in Victoria Park and go well fed and warmly clad, whilst the children of those grey slums were lacking the very necessities of life.

When Richard Pankhurst died suddenly in 1898 his wife and their three young daughters – Christabel, Sylvia and Adela – wanted to carry on the public service and community spirit he had developed, and which his family shared and supported. One of the principles he taught his daughters was this: *"If you do not work for others, you will not have been worth the upbringing."* Christabel – and Sylvia in particular – took this to heart. Many years later Sylvia's son said of his mother that everything she undertook she entered into with total commitment, without counting the cost to herself.

Richard Pankhurst's widow, Emmeline, was beautiful, elegant and romantic. She was also an intelligent woman, and unusually outspoken for the times in which she lived, even before she became a crusader for women's suffrage.

Emmeline Pankhurst was born in 1858, so she had grown up at a time when most middle-class women had led highly restricted lives. Respectable women (and being respectable was critically important) lived within the tight confines of conventional family life. The rules that governed women's behaviour in the 1800s were strict, clear and comprehensive. They covered almost every social situation and included guidance for every social class. For example, no respectable middle-class woman would leave her house without wearing a hat with a veil that covered at least the top half of her face. No respectable woman of any class would be seen in public with a man who was not her husband, father or brother.

Of course, there were other women in Britain who were far from respectable – prostitutes, for example, or women who had children without being married. Such women were treated as moral outcasts and condemned by all. Their desperate predicament was used as a frightening example to respectable women; their desolate situations showed what happened to women who flouted society's rules. There wasn't any space between those two moral extremes – in Victorian society you were either acceptable, or you were not. Women could get dangerous and low-paid factory work or work as domestic servants, or even perhaps as governesses if their class and education made that possible. But there was nothing else.

By the time Sylvia Pankhurst was growing up at the end of the nineteenth century, girls from middle-class families were still expected simply to learn how to be good wives and mothers, as their own mothers had done. They were certainly not encouraged – and generally were not even permitted – to get a good education or even to think or act for themselves. Their fathers, brothers, and later (if they married) their husbands, were expected to think for them and act on their behalf.

The way in which Emmeline's three daughters were raised and educated was both progressive and exceptional for the times. All three of them attended Manchester High School, and both Christabel and Sylvia went on to further education. Most girls were taught to read and write but the rest of their education concentrated on domestic skills. They learned to sew and embroider and manage a household, and girls from well-to-do families also learned to dance and sing, and perhaps to play the piano. They were taught deportment, and how to behave in a decorous and polite way – speaking in low voices, and never arguing or even laughing in public.

The brothers of these girls were sent to school or tutored privately at home, and learned a wide range of classical subjects as well as some scientific and mathematical ones. But girls were not expected to use their brains.

In general, women were seen as *"mild, soft and amiable"*, while men had to be *"practical, stable and superior of intellect"*. Mr Bumble, a character in Charles Dickens's nineteenth-century novel, *Oliver Twist*, put it like this: *"the prerogative of a man is to command ... the prerogative of a woman is to obey."* And another contemporary writer said:

When I speak of the women of England I have in my mind those young, pure-minded girls who are the light and life of their homes: who develop into the wives and mothers of England: who bring up England's children in the fear of God, and in the love of all that is pure and good: who bless the homes of which they are the pride and comfort.

So it was not just voting that was forbidden – Victorian women had very few rights of any kind. Despite the fact that a woman (Queen Victoria) was on the throne from 1837 until she died in 1901, British women were expected to defer to men about almost everything. Until 1870, for example, women who owned property lost control of it when they married – anything they owned automatically became their husbands' property. (So most of the women who had qualified to vote in local elections because they owned property were either unmarried, or widows.) If a married woman had a job, not only would she earn less than half of what a man would get for the same job, but the money she earned would legally belong to her husband and not to her. In fact, a woman's husband was her legal "keeper" – which meant that her body, her earnings, her children and her domestic services belonged to him.

Progress on any aspect of equal rights for women was very slow, although at the end of the nineteenth century a few pioneers successfully challenged some accepted ideas about a woman's place. Florence Nightingale organized a nursing service that inspired many young women to become nurses, Elizabeth Garrett Anderson opened a dispensary in London and later practised as a doctor, and a group of women founded a university college in Cambridge (Girton College) that women could attend. (Even after Girton College was founded women could not be awarded university degrees until 1878 – at Oxford it was not until 1928.) These advances did begin to change the view of what women should and shouldn't – and could and couldn't – do.

After Richard Pankhurst died, Emmeline Pankhurst needed to earn money to help support her family, and took part-time work as a registrar of births and deaths in a working-class area in Manchester. There she saw for herself the conditions in which such women lived and worked, and how badly they needed the power that voting would give them. She began to think of votes for women – of women's suffrage – not only as a right, but also as a desperate necessity.

The word "suffrage" comes from the Latin word *suffragium*, meaning "vote". In English, suffrage means "the *right* to vote" – so women's suffrage means the right for women to vote and a suffragist is someone (man or woman) who believes in the right to vote. For Emmeline Pankhurst and her daughters, women's suffrage became the most important thing in the world and the overriding passion of their lives.

As it happened, their timing was right, too. By 1900, just two years after Richard Pankhurst's death, the suffrage movement in Britain began to stir. Women had been campaigning for the vote since the 1860s, and Millicent Fawcett had formed the National Union of Women's Suffrage Societies (NUWSS) in 1897. Now local suffrage societies became more active again. Some women's suffrage supporters even argued that women's right to vote was not a new right at all. They pointed out that it had existed for women in the past, and had been unjustly removed by the wording of the reform acts in the 1800s. These people now began to insist that the right to vote should be *returned* to British women.

The reform law of 1884 had given the vote to many men who didn't own property, and in some cases – for example, with agricultural labourers – these men had never had a chance to learn to read or write. That situation outraged middle-class women who longed for the right to vote. They believed that the great prize of suffrage had been tossed to a group of men far less qualified than they were – the excluded property-owning women. If the politicians of the day could give illiterate working men the vote, they said, how could it possibly be fair to continue to deny it to educated, middle-class women?

But opposition to women's suffrage was strong and it included many women – even Queen Victoria thought it was a *"wicked folly"* for women to want the vote. She said that Lady Amberley, who had been brave enough to address a suffrage meeting, *"ought to get a good whipping"*. Many anti-suffragists believed that women were less intelligent and less able to make political decisions than men. They argued that men could represent their wives and daughters better than those women could represent themselves. Others feared that women's participation in politics would lead to the end of family life. And almost every political party in the country opposed women's suffrage.

Some women in Britain accepted their powerless situation because they had never known anything else. Most of them had probably never even thought of voting, and some certainly agreed with the men who believed that women should not vote. Those who did support the idea of women's suffrage, and who found the situation unjust, might try to argue or write against it, but any woman who dared to call for equal rights was thought strange and shocking. British women had been trained to avoid being conspicuous, and to have a horror of being gossiped about in polite society. And although women had no hope of advancing their rights *without* flouting such rules, it took enormous courage for them to take a radical stand about anything. Emmeline Pankhurst certainly possessed that courage – and so did her daughters.

Millicent Fawcett's National Union of Women's Suffrage Societies (NUWSS) was the largest suffrage organization in Britain, and would always remain so. But with the help and support of her daughters, and with the encouragement of a growing number of women in Britain, Emmeline founded a new women's suffrage organization in 1903. It was called the Women's Social and Political Union (the WSPU), and it had the motto *"Deeds Not Words"*. The WSPU was determined to make its own distinctive mark.

Sylvia Pankhurst and her sister Christabel were both involved in the WSPU from the start. Emmeline Pankhurst particularly relied on Christabel to help her build the new organization – Christabel was glamorous, a fiery speaker, and the one who regularly captured attention. In contrast Sylvia seemed quiet and shy, *"a plain little woman"* as one report dismissively said. But she quickly showed how important her work for the WSPU would be.

In the first two years of the WSPU Emmeline and Christabel did most of the groundwork. Sylvia, a talented artist, had won a scholarship to the Royal College of Art in London, so she moved away from her

Manchester home. At first Sylvia was desperately lonely in London, away from her family and friends. But she enjoyed her work at the college and she saw her brother Henry – at boarding school in Hampstead – every second Sunday. Sylvia also spent time with Keir Hardie, the leader of the Independent Labour Party, who had been her father's friend. It was at this time that Sylvia joined Keir Hardie's party. Their close friendship gradually deepened to love, but Keir Hardie was already married, so he and Sylvia kept their feelings secret. Despite those difficulties they gave each other steadfast and loyal support for many years.

When the new session of parliament opened in 1905 Emmeline Pankhurst came to London to lobby Members of Parliament (MPs) about women's suffrage; to try to get them to change their minds and support votes for women.

Supporters of women's suffrage knew the main problem was trying to change the law. It's one thing to try to change a law if you have a vote. Your MPs will want to listen to your arguments, because they know you can vote against them if you choose. But if you don't have the power of a vote to back you, how can you persuade MPs to listen to you? How can you convert them to your cause?

Ever since the reform law of 1867 had excluded women from its definition of the "*persons*" who could vote, regular deputations of women's suffrage supporters had lobbied parliament. These annual deputations had achieved very little more than a game of mutual good manners with the parliamentarians. The women arrived at Westminster, and were escorted into the parliament buildings to be given afternoon tea by MPs. The suffrage supporters argued their case: the MPs listened to them politely. Then the women departed and the MPs returned to the real business of their working lives – supporting the policies of their political parties. And since those policies did not include giving women the vote, the delegations did not achieve very much. The male MPs knew they did not *have* to attend to the women, or do what they wanted. So even the few MPs who were sympathetic to women's suffrage did not put it at the top of their "to do" lists.

That pattern of inaction was the very one that Emmeline Pankhurst and the WSPU now hoped to change. Emmeline stayed with Sylvia, involved her in everything, and swept her along to meetings and discussions. Sylvia's rooms in South Kensington were suddenly filled with WSPU visitors, and her art studies soon took a back seat. She later wrote of that time, "*my life was changed for ever*". It was a memorable transformation.

Election Fever

WHEN THE EXPECTED election was finally called in the autumn of 1905, thousands of women took a new and personal interest in politics as they had never done before. After all the years of difficulty and stagnation, it suddenly looked as though a time of destiny for women's suffrage was just over the horizon. Everyone thought the Conservative government was going to fall from power at the end of the year, and that a new Liberal government would be elected in its place.

Not all Liberal politicians were committed to women's suffrage, but many of them said they were. And if the Liberal Party was in power in the House of Commons with a strong majority, then a women's suffrage bill might be supported by the new government and finally become law.

Asquith, together with other Liberal Party members such as Edward Grey and Winston Churchill, spoke at countless political rallies. (Churchill was then a member of the Liberal Party, although he later joined the Conservative Party.) The Liberals wanted to convince voters that the world would be infinitely better when the Conservatives were swept away and a new Liberal government took their place.

Wherever the Liberal politicians spoke, however, a new phenomenon occurred. Women in the audience leapt to their feet wanting to speak, or called out questions to the candidates. They demanded – sometimes politely, but always persistently – to be told what the politicians on the platform thought about votes for women. What would the Liberal Party do to help women's suffrage?

The politicians didn't want to answer that question. They didn't want to be committed to supporting it because they knew their party didn't have a firm position about it, and it was a contentious and difficult issue. But of course they didn't usually want to say no, either!

The women's interventions were initially supposed simply to make a point, and try to focus political attention on the suffrage issue. Most of the women asked their questions politely, but some of them wouldn't give up easily. They shouted even louder if they were ignored or dismissed, and kicked up a fuss in public, as women never had before. Usually a few Liberal Party stewards managed to grab the noisy protesters and throw them out into the street: but still, it was a strange and unsettling development; all very surprising for the politicians, and very undignified.

Asquith could not believe that votes for women would come that way – through noisy protests and unmannerly interventions – and for himself, he hoped they would never come at all. But he did not yet take the matter very seriously. He concentrated all his efforts on getting himself – and other Liberals – elected. Asquith had given up the last of his legal practice, and thrown himself completely into political life. His whole future was at stake.

Asquith was poised to take power in government again and his opposition remained implacable. Those of his friends who supported women's suffrage found his opposition to it a mystery, for they knew Asquith as a clever, good-tempered man and a sophisticated, worldly person. He was certainly not a fool. Surely, they thought, he could understand the progressive view? He was a leading Liberal Party politician, and the Liberals supported reform – surely Asquith could support this reform for women?

But in fact Asquith did not even want the vote extended to include more men, let alone to women as well. He was a rising star in the Liberal Party and committed to many reforms, but he was also a very proper and old-fashioned man, and held rather traditional views about society. Reform was one thing: profound social change was another, and he put women's suffrage in the second category. In fact, Asquith was always suspicious of extremes, especially if they were argued for in violent ways. And he hated and mistrusted emotional displays in public life, taking pride in always using rational arguments rather than emotional ones.

In 1905, opposition to women's suffrage was regarded as the norm. If you were against votes for women, you were in the majority. Prominent professional men, and many important women, agreed that women should *not* have the vote – did not need to vote – and, it was claimed, did not even truly *want* to vote. Women were unfit to make political decisions, thundered Sir Almroth Wright, a famous doctor – menstruation and the menopause made women unstable, and thus unable to be trusted with the nation's business. He was not alone in that opinion: many men agreed with him.

Others stressed the dangers to society if women lost their feminine nature – their "*charm of modesty*" or their "*grace of dignified reserve*" through undertaking political activities. (The truth was, many working-class women already did "unfeminine" work in fields, factories and coal mines: this argument really applied only to middle- and upper-class women who were expected to be ladies, and do nothing in particular.) Mary Humphrey Ward, a leading anti-suffragist and the first president of the Anti-Suffrage League, wrote that men's problems could only be solved by men. "*Constitutional, legal, financial and military problems,*" she said, needed the "*special knowledge*" of men, who ought to be "*left unhampered by the political inexperience of women*". G.K. Chesterton, a famous poet and writer, answered this ironically in the *Illustrated London News* magazine by saying:

> ...if voting is only putting a cross against certain names, then certainly women could do it as well as men... But voting, if it means anything, means doing all the things that males have always done – notably, fighting, drinking, and talking about everything and nothing.

Women were not educated to undertake political activity, went another argument. One woman suffragist countered that claim very neatly. *"Then in God's name give women the suffrage quickly,"* she replied, *"for only then will men see the necessity of educating them."*

A general dislike of change was at the core of anti-suffrage opinion in Britain. Many people – women as well as men – believed that British society was already organized in the right way, and they did not want it to change. Giving the vote to millions of women would alter everyone's lives in ways that seemed alarmingly unpredictable and dangerous, as well as unnecessary. The idea struck at the heart of everything, at the way in which people saw themselves. So it is not surprising that it met with resistance.

By the time of the election campaign at the end of 1905, these old arguments against women voting had begun to look shabby and outdated, and women were finally beginning to assert themselves. Asquith, however, held firmly to his beliefs. He was not going to be swayed by any passing fashion, and he was not alone in his opposition to women's suffrage within his political party.

Some Liberal politicians believed that women were naturally conservative thinkers, and they feared that enfranchised women [women who could vote] would probably vote for the Conservative Party, rather than for the Liberals. Many Conservative politicians as well as Liberals resisted women's suffrage just because it would change the balance of power in the country in ways they could not predict. Unless politicians were confident that the new women voters were likely to support their party, they didn't want to extend the vote to them. And some politicians also believed that when it came to it, British men would not accept women's suffrage simply because it would put women voters in a majority.

There were also many long-standing political causes that Liberals wished to support, more important to them than the abolition of sex-discrimination in the voting regulations. (Two central Liberal aims at this time were limiting the power of the House of Lords – which could successfully block any government legislation that it opposed – and Home Rule for Ireland, which was then entirely governed from London. Asquith was instrumental in the Liberal Party's struggle to achieve those goals.) Even if they did support women's suffrage, most Liberal MPs thought women should wait in line patiently for their turn to come – whenever that might be – while those like Asquith who opposed it made every possible effort to dismiss and ignore the issue, or to keep it on the sidelines.

Some suffrage supporters thought that neither the Liberals nor the Conservatives would ever give women votes. They saw the new Labour Party as a much better bet. Labour Party candidates and supporters often drew a picture of a future and wonderful world with women voters, women Members of Parliament, and women in all the professions. This radical vision made the Labour Party very attractive to supporters of women's rights.

But many Labour politicians believed that supporting universal adult suffrage – votes for all adults, both men and women, rather than only for some women – was the best way forward. They saw that the remaining suffrage inequalities in Britain – the adults who were still denied the vote – included many men as well as all women. The Labour Party supported two voting reforms: women's suffrage, and universal adult suffrage. Some Labour members thought women's suffrage should come first: others believed that universal adult suffrage should come first. It seemed to be a question of priorities.

Women campaigners often suspected – and sometimes with good reason – that *"universal adult suffrage"* was a convenient slogan for those who didn't really care if women voted or not. Those women suspected that the Labour Party was more interested in universal *male* suffrage. Christabel Pankhurst spoke out against automatic support for the Labour Party. *"Why are women expected to have such confidence in the men of the Labour Party?"* she wrote. *"Working men are as unjust to women as are those of other classes."* And even though Sylvia was a Labour Party supporter, even she was not sure that Labour would provide a solution.

The election gave the Liberal Party a huge majority in the House of Commons of nearly 100 members, and so they formed the new government. Henry Campbell-Bannerman became the new Prime Minister, and he appointed Asquith as Chancellor of the Exchequer (in charge of the country's finances). It was a triumph, and gave Asquith the second most important job in British politics, at the heart of the new government's power.

Pankhurst
Deeds Not Words
1906

THE ELECTION WAS exciting for women's suffrage supporters, too. As well as the Liberal success, more than 30 Labour Party members were also elected to parliament, and they were pledged to support the Liberal Party. Now there were a total of 420 MPs, belonging to all the political parties, who said they supported women's suffrage. Perhaps votes for women could at last be achieved. Surely all it would take now was one last push...

Votes for women! Those words – that shout of determination – now started to build into a chorus up and down the country, and the WSPU had been encouraged by the statements made by some Liberal candidates during the election campaign. Now Sylvia Pankhurst, as the WSPU representative in London, tried to arrange for a delegation to talk to the new Prime Minister about

suffrage. She wrote to him at the beginning of 1906 on behalf of the WSPU, asking him to meet them.

However, Sir Henry Campbell-Bannerman was not convinced by the arguments about women's suffrage. He had not made his opposition public as Asquith had, but he was certainly no supporter of women's suffrage. So he chose to ignore the demands made by women's suffrage organizations. When he got Sylvia's letter he snubbed her, and replied loftily that he could not spare the time to meet the WSPU.

It started to look as though the Liberal Party leaders would not give women any help unless they were forced to. The suffrage organizations were especially angry about Asquith's adamant opposition. As Chancellor, Asquith was responsible for deciding how much tax they paid – but at the same time he denied them political representation. The women argued that taxing people who did not have a vote was immoral. Several times that year, members of the WSPU tried to disrupt meetings where he was speaking.

Later that year the Labour Party conference gave universal adult suffrage priority, as their main target. Some Labour politicians still believed that women's suffrage should be the party's main aim, and the Labour leader, Keir Hardie, remained committed to that. But even Hardie's arguments did not alter the Labour Party's decision. Now it seemed that no political party in the national parliament at Westminster would give priority to the women's cause.

There was another problem. The newspapers of the time, taking their lead from influential politicians, often ignored the women's suffrage organizations. It was no longer extraordinary or newsworthy to report on a woman speaking in public or a group of women arriving at the Houses of Parliament with a petition, as it had been a few years earlier. The women knew it was tremendously important for them to get the country's attention: they had to turn their issue into a national debate and engage the interest of both parliament and the newspapers. But how?

The Pankhursts' WSPU was based in Manchester, and its activities had been organized from there since its formation. But in order to succeed nationally the WSPU needed to raise its profile. It had to attract the attention of the politicians and national newspapers that were based in London. It had to find ways to be noticed.

The WSPU decided on a dramatic campaign. Other women's suffrage groups, such as the NUWSS, didn't alter their campaign methods at all. They stayed relatively inconspicuous and well-behaved, and kept on doing what they had always done – working hard to bring the opposition around to their point of view through argument and persuasion. They believed that any change of tactics would do their cause more harm than good.

But the WSPU said that quiet tactics – the patience and moderation that had been used until now – had done little to change the politicians. If the men in power continued to ignore the issue, then the women *without* power would have to do something more to grab their attention. They decided to use more aggressive, militant tactics.

Because Sylvia was living in London, studying art at the Royal College, she was the obvious choice to lead a London-based campaign. Emmeline had returned to Manchester after lobbying parliament; Christabel was also based in that city. But Annie Kenney, a mill girl and a prominent member of the WSPU in Manchester (and the only working-class woman in the WSPU leadership), travelled to London to join Sylvia. Together the two young women planned their assault on London.

Sylvia and Annie chose to organize a meeting and a march on the parliament buildings at Westminster. They timed it to mark the opening of the new parliamentary session, and highlight the lack of representation for women. They resolved to get as many suffrage supporters as possible to march with them, and they also decided on something that no one had done before. Ignoring the old class divisions, Sylvia and Annie would persuade hundreds of working-class women from London's East End to join them. They would rouse the *whole* of London's women!

It was an ambitious aim. Many London suffragists who supported the more conventional NUWSS didn't believe the newcomers could do so much in only a few weeks.

Even Emmeline Pankhurst was alarmed when she learned of their plan. In the past, most middle-class women had come to suffrage meetings in their carriages, clapped their neatly gloved hands politely when agreement and applause were required, and then returned home to have tea and discuss the meeting in a private and ladylike way. They had certainly left any marching or demonstrating to a few daring enthusiasts.

But everyone underestimated Sylvia's determination and Annie's energy, as well as their political cleverness. Sylvia thought the NUWSS was too staid, too willing to wait, and far too leisurely in its approach. She thought this was an excellent chance to show what could be done instead.

Together Sylvia and Annie interviewed newspaper editors, booked a large London hall, planned the procession route, and advertised the whole event. Sylvia got Keir Hardie's help to plan their tactics, and used the Labour Party's local branches to publicize her appeal to working women. Now there could be no turning back! On 16 February 1906, more than 300 women from the East End marched from St James Park underground station to Caxton Hall for the meeting, and then almost all the women who had gathered – more than 1,000 of them in all – marched through the streets together to Westminster!

One London member of the NUWSS described her impressions to a friend. The women who marched, she said:

...would have nothing to do with any of the old-established Suffrage Societies, they met under the Labour Party with their own flags and carrying their own babies.

She concluded: *"New winds are blowing through society."* She was right.

The national newspapers – the ones that had apparently decided that the NUWSS had become too boring to report – couldn't ignore the appeal of the WSPU actions. The sheer excitement and exuberance of the new approach caught their imagination, and reports of the march as well as interviews with Sylvia and Annie filled their pages. It was around this time that the *Daily Mail* newspaper invented the word *"suffragette"*. Some of the women who fought for the vote preferred the word *"suffragist"*, because they thought *"suffragette"* was intended to sound patronizing with its *"ette"* ending. It probably was. But suffragette was the word that almost everyone began to use, and that people still use today when these events are described. And, as Sylvia Pankhurst said, at least the press was finally sitting up and taking notice.

▦

Encouraged by success, the WSPU started to increase its activities. Its members were instructed to conduct the biggest publicity campaign ever seen – to make it, in Emmeline Pankhurst's words, *"more colourful and more commanding of attention than anything ever seen before"*. And one of their first targets was the Liberal Party. The WSPU tried once again to force a meeting with the Prime Minister, to convince him of the justice of giving women the vote. Other suffrage organizations supported the WSPU and decided to join in. In October 1906 they arranged to meet the WSPU delegation at Westminster, outside the Houses of Parliament.

The WSPU, however, continued to develop their spirited flair for publicity. They decided to assemble on the Thames Embankment by the statue of Boudicca, the famous warrior queen of the ancient Britons. Then they marched to Westminster to meet the other delegations and confront Campbell-Bannerman. The meeting that assembled in Trafalgar Square after the meeting with the Prime Minister attracted a crowd of about 7,000 supporters.

By this stage, each of the women's suffrage organizations was developing its own set of colours. The WSPU colours were purple for dignity, white for purity and green for hope for the future: the NUWSS colours were red, white and green. Every suffrage organisation encouraged its supporters to wear clothes, sashes and badges that supported the campaign, and shops soon opened throughout Britain to sell such materials. So meetings and marches like this one were already bright with the colours of suffrage loyalty.

Converting the Country

Asquith

1906

THIS TIME THE PRIME MINISTER decided he would see the suffrage delegation. An envoy of 300 women, who represented more than 125,000 suffragists (both men and women) crowded into a hall to hear what he had to say to them. Sir Henry Campbell-Bannerman told the delegation he agreed with their arguments – but, he added, "*I propose to do nothing at all about it.*" He could, he explained, do nothing to help while significant members of his Cabinet were still opposed to it. (The Cabinet is the group of MPs who hold office under a Prime Minister, and so help to lead the government.) Even though Campbell-Bannerman claimed that he himself was in favour of women's suffrage, the new Liberal government did not plan, he said, to initiate any legislation for votes for women.

Henry Campbell-Bannerman also suggested to the delegation that they should continue "*pestering*" and

41

"converting the country". In the world he knew, which was ruled by convention and restraint, this might have been perfectly sensible political advice. But it was not welcomed by the delegates who heard it, and in the new world where militant women were willing to flout convention and throw off social restraints, it was also remarkably unwise advice.

The Prime Minister did not, of course, realize how his suggestion of *"pestering"* might be interpreted. He believed that only an enormous swell of popular opinion in Britain would move his colleagues in parliament to take women's suffrage seriously. He probably privately thought the same himself – that if *he* was going to be persuaded to take the suffragettes seriously they would first have to show him a convinced British public.

Sir Henry Campbell-Bannerman did not expect the WSPU to choose militant methods in order to *"convert the country"*, nor did he expect or approve the violent results that followed – like Asquith, he abhorred both things. But the Prime Minister made the further mistake of lecturing the delegation on the *"virtue of patience"*. Since some of the women to whom he spoke had been working for women's rights for almost 50 years, that was both patronizing and infuriating. Annie Kenney, who was one of the delegates, jumped to her feet and then on to a chair in the hall. *"Sir,"* she cried angrily, *"we are not satisfied!"* It was offensive to counsel patience to mill girls like Annie, who urgently needed a solution to the problems they faced daily in their work. Without the power of the vote, working women like Annie knew they could not improve their working lives.

The Prime Minister's comments about other members of his Cabinet confirmed the suffragettes' suspicions that Asquith was their main enemy. The WSPU next asked to meet with him, but he refused to do so. He had already been the target of some protest, but from then on Asquith became the sustained focus of militant action.

Rise Up, Women!

AT FIRST, THE WSPU's militancy might seem to us to be rather tame – but for the times, the tactics were both radical and effective. Women from all social classes, but mostly from the middle class, attended public meetings where Asquith was due to speak, and interrupted the proceedings by calling out protests or slogans. The women knew their behaviour would probably result in their being booed and shouted at, and that if they persisted they would probably be dragged out of the meeting in a humiliating way – manhandled by Asquith's supporters. For women who had until then lived very sheltered lives, those experiences were entirely new as well as shocking and unpleasant, but they quickly became accustomed to them. And at first, that was what *"militant action"* meant, and that was just about the worst that happened.

There is no doubt that being committed to a cause, and being part of a movement to bring about change, is very exciting for those involved. The suffragettes were certainly no exception. More and more women began to join suffrage societies and take part in the protest movement. By this time, the *"Votes for Women"* campaign was often simply referred to as *"The Cause"*.

Quite quickly, too, many women became accustomed to behaving in a completely different way to the one in which they had been brought up. They marched through the streets with banners and flags calling for votes for women, and found they didn't very much mind being labelled *"brazen"* by the newspapers, or mocked by passers-by. They wrote, illustrated, printed and issued leaflets and handbills that called for women to unite: Sylvia's artistic training was often called on, and the poster designs she produced at this time were very popular. And in increasing numbers, the suffragettes called for other women to unite with them in opposition to Asquith and the rest of the Liberal Party government.

Such events, such discussions and actions, had not been witnessed in Britain before. Respectable women did not march through the streets! Polite society did not permit such behaviour: it was scandalous! Women who demonstrated in public places risked a great deal. They risked their reputations and their employment if they had jobs. They risked being mocked and ridiculed by passers-by as they stood or marched in the streets. They even risked being arrested by policemen.

Those risks were unpleasant but the women's public demonstrations created a shock wave that rolled through society, and that was exactly what the protesters wanted. Publicity was their goal – it was what the WSPU needed. If you achieve the effect you long for, then the risks you have taken often seem to have been worth any amount of pain and struggle. And if you achieve the desired results, you will also be encouraged to keep going.

At the beginning of 1907 the leaders of the suffrage societies combined to organize an open-air procession through the streets of London. They wanted to demonstrate mass support for votes for women, and in spite of heavy rain about 4,000 people turned out for it.

The march was later called the Mud March because of the weather that day. It might not sound important or even especially memorable that it was raining that day and that the streets were muddy. But if you were a middle-class or upper-class woman marching in 1907 you would be wearing a long skirt – long enough to touch the ground. Most women marchers ended up with soaked and muddy skirts that day. (Younger women, like Sylvia Pankhurst, wore skirts that were shorter and came just above their ankles. They wanted to be able to move easily, walk fast, and show they didn't support the old ways. Working-class women and especially household servants also wore shorter skirts. If their skirts had touched the ground they'd never have been able to carry things up and down stairs without tripping, as they needed to do in their jobs.)

Three days later, on the day the new session of Parliament opened, the WSPU held what they called a women's parliament meeting to highlight their lack of representation in parliament. The atmosphere was tense in the meeting hall as the women waited to hear what was in the King's Speech then being announced in parliament. That would tell the country what the Liberal government wanted to achieve in the next session. The news came: there was no mention of women's suffrage at all. Clearly, the Liberal Party planned to continue to ignore women's suffrage.

"Rise up, women!" cried Emmeline Pankhurst, leaping to her feet, and back came an enormous shout from the assembled women – *"Now!"* Four hundred women streamed out of the hall and marched to Westminster. As the head of the march reached Westminster Abbey the women were confronted by mounted police who told them they could not present a petition to parliament: they must turn back. The women refused. Mounted police then rode their horses directly into the march and straight at the ranks of women, scattering them and knocking many of them to the ground. Then police on foot seized those on the ground and rushed them out of the way, hitting them as they went. Again and again the women tried to re-form their ranks; again and again the mounted police charged them. Those who

took refuge in doorways were dragged out and pounced on by police again.

The battle lasted for hours. Sylvia and Christabel were among 54 women who were arrested for their part in it.

Even the usually hostile newspapers were shocked by what had happened in Parliament Square. When reports of it were published the public were dismayed at the police tactics. Many MPs – even those who did not support the women's cause – believed that a settlement must be reached with the suffragettes right away, before things got any worse. A group of MPs immediately drafted a Women's Suffrage Bill. This bill was uncomplicated in its approach, and simply aimed to alter the interpretation of the "*male persons*" words from the Reform Bills of the previous century. It proposed that in every law that regulated voting qualifications, "*male persons*" should be assumed to include women. In addition, the bill said that women should not be disqualified from voting by getting married.

However, as soon as the Women's Suffrage Bill was debated in the House of Commons all the old difficulties and arguments came to life again. Many MPs like Asquith simply opposed it. The bill would do nothing for working-class women, so other Liberal and Labour Party MPs who might have been sympathetic did not support it either. Campbell-Bannerman, the Prime Minister, said he would vote for it but he wouldn't make it official

Liberal Party policy to do so – he knew how deeply divided his party was on the matter. Other Liberals said they would rather wait for a new and properly drafted reform bill that dealt more intelligently with the suffrage issues.

"Why does there have to be such a fight? Such a struggle to win a just cause?" asked Annie Kenney. *"There seems to be such hypocrisy, such insincerity, such lying and such a lot of humbug."* It was all so insulting to suffragettes who were eager to get on with their other interests and causes, and whose lives would be so much better with the power of the vote behind them. The failure of the politicians to take women seriously was a frustration that seemed without remedy.

And the Women's Suffrage Bill failed.

This Must End!

In the House of Commons there were discussions, promises and evasions on women's suffrage, but nothing more. Outside the House there was an ever-growing clamour. More and more frequently, Members of Parliament – and especially members of the Liberal government like Asquith – were attacked in public when they spoke at political meetings.

MPs were not accustomed to disrespectful treatment in public – such as having bags of flour thrown at them in the middle of a speech to a hall of supporters. They were confused and bewildered by this approach, and frequently also very angry. To the women it was almost a game, although it was a dangerous one. To the MPs, it represented enormous loss of face, and the risk of public humiliation. They did everything they could to stop it.

The meeting organizers grew more used to the women's tactics as time passed. The meeting stewards learned to pick out possible troublemakers amongst the women in the audience, but sometimes they completely failed to mark their targets – who were often such mild and respectable-looking women!

But now as soon as such a protest began – as soon as any woman at all stood to ask a question or called out from the body of the hall – the meeting stewards or other male supporters would pounce on her and drag her out of the meeting. But as they did so, other voices suddenly called out from around the hall in a shout of *"Votes for women!"* Stink bombs, rattles and hand-bells would taunt the frantic stewards, who rushed to try to restore order.

Each meeting would fall further into chaos, with walking sticks and dog whips lashing through the air as other male members of the audience took out their frustration on the women protesters, or on each other. Finally almost the entire audience would be yelling sympathy or abuse, helping with the chucking-out, or hurling themselves on to the stewards. The hall would become completely consumed by the fight, rather than by the subject of the meeting. As often as not, yet another Liberal Party event would be ruined or closed down.

Despite the recent failures in the House of Commons, it still seemed right for women to aim their suffrage efforts at MPs. That is how change had been brought about in the recent past, and many of the women who supported women's suffrage in a less militant fashion based their tactics on past experience of changing other laws. For example, in the early 1800s women had organized an effective campaign against slavery. Antislavery groups had put pressure on individual MPs, had held public meetings to argue their case and raise funds, and had gathered signatures for petitions that were then presented to politicians. And the campaign had succeeded – slavery had finally been outlawed in Britain and its colonies, under a Liberal government.

So supporters of women's suffrage knew they had to use parliament to change the law. All laws were made and changed in parliament, as they still are today. The problem was to know how to persuade MPs to change their minds. Many individual MPs supported women's suffrage, but in practice there were not enough of them to get more than a narrow majority in a parliamentary vote. That was not sufficient to support a new law that gave women the vote. When it came to the crunch, some MPs who said they supported women's suffrage wouldn't vote in favour of it. Other MPs were prevented from voting in favour of women's suffrage by their political parties.

Women's suffrage supporters still tried to get their cause debated in parliament. They reasoned that if the issue was supported by a large enough majority of MPs, then perhaps it could be turned into law: perhaps more

MPs could be converted by argument. So suffrage societies regularly tried to persuade sympathetic MPs to debate the matter in the House of Commons, and pushed for a bill to be drafted and supported by one of the political parties. If the government could be persuaded to add a Women's Suffrage Bill to their list, there was a good chance of it going forward.

Many suffrage groups pressed individual MPs for their help. At the beginning of every parliamentary session, MPs entered a ballot for the right to introduce a bill of their own. If the suffrage groups got enough MPs to agree to put forward a private member's bill for them, and if just one of those MPs was lucky enough to win the ballot – well then, they stood a chance of success.

There was very little time for an individual MP to introduce a private bill, and very little chance that he could get enough support from other MPs to vote it into law. (The British parliament in Westminster still has ballots for private members' bills, and it is still very difficult for such a bill to become law.)

The difficulties didn't stop suffrage groups from trying. They tried year after year to have some sort of women's suffrage bill introduced into the House of Commons by an individual MP, or by an independent group of MPs. But every time, the bill failed to get through. There were (and still are) many ways for MPs to block a bill they don't support. For example, in 1905, before the election, MPs like Asquith and his supporters had not even bothered to speak against the current private member's bill on women's suffrage. They simply made sure that other parliamentary business took so much time there was none left for the suffrage bill. They just talked it out.

▦

In October 1907 Asquith told a deputation of women who met him in his East Fife constituency that he was still an anti-suffragist. The following month Keir Hardie introduced a Women's Enfranchisement Bill in parliament, as a private member's bill. The bill would give women the vote, and introducing it gave the Labour Party leader the chance to criticize the Prime Minister and his Cabinet for their stand against women's suffrage. But the bill couldn't proceed because the government would not make room for it in the parliamentary business.

Even MPs who supported women's suffrage argued with each other about *which* women should be allowed to vote. Should it be all women over a certain age – perhaps 30? Or should it be only women who owned property? And those questions threw up yet more arguments. If all *women* over 30, for example, were to be allowed to vote, shouldn't all *men* over 30 also be allowed to vote? This argument made universal adult suffrage, not just women's suffrage, the central issue. Women themselves often disagreed about the issue. Social class – which was much more important in 1905 than it is now – divided them and affected their thinking. So some middle-class women didn't think that working women should have a vote, any more than they thought that working *men* should vote. And at first many women were divided – as were men – by their party affiliation, their religious beliefs and their political outlook.

When women realized how many ways there were for a bill on women's suffrage to be blocked, they knew private members' bills were useless to them. If legislation was ever going to be passed, it needed the support of at least one political party – and preferably the one in power. But many Liberal politicians did not believe in women's suffrage themselves – and, like Asquith, they didn't believe that a majority of women in Britain wanted the vote, either. Perhaps, they said amongst themselves, it was just a few noisy extremists who wanted it. If that were true, it wouldn't help the Liberal Party to stay in power if they supported the demands of extremist cranks.

In the meantime the suffragettes stepped up their public protests, and took their actions to another level. Asquith's home in a sedate London square had been targeted in June 1907. Groups of women from London's East End marched around the square with banners. The rest of the square's residents were horrified – what were these working-class women doing in their part of town? Cavendish Square was the home of the rich and the aristocratic – working-class women had no business there except as servants. The police were called.

The women rang Asquith's front-door bell, and refused to leave. They knew Asquith himself wasn't at home but they were determined to make their point. Several women were then arrested and removed – but another band of women then took over. When the police arrested them as well, members of Asquith's family – and some of the servants in the house – appeared at the windows to clap and cheer the police efforts. It was all very unusual.

The women who were arrested refused to pay the fines that the court imposed on them. The magistrate remonstrated with the women. *"This shall come to an end,"* he said. *"It must come to an end! I shall bring it to an end!"* He imprisoned them for periods ranging from six weeks to two months in London's Holloway Prison for Women, but he did not succeed in bringing their protests to an end.

War of the Women
1908

DELIBERATELY CHOOSING imprisonment – going out of their way to get arrested, not resisting arrest, and refusing to pay fines – was a radical step for the women. The WSPU broke with traditional suffrage campaigning when its members made that decision. It was a startling move, and an outrageously successful way to capture public attention. Now, selected WSPU members actually volunteered to provoke imprisonment by breaking the law.

The other suffrage movements such as the NUWSS did not join them in that. Even the WSPU leadership were taken by surprise by the new tactic. The first time that it happened, Emmeline Pankhurst did not understand that the arrested members wanted to be imprisoned, and rushed to pay the fines so as to release them. Her offer was angrily refused.

In the early days, the law-breaking involved only technical breaches of minor laws – for example, women were arrested for slapping or spitting at policemen who were attempting to break up their demonstrations. When they were charged and brought to court for assault the women scornfully refused to pay a fine, and so they were sentenced to prison for a short time instead.

Christabel Pankhurst, Sylvia's older sister, had first introduced this shock tactic several years before, during the 1905 election campaign. A small group of women, including Christabel Pankhurst and Annie Kenney, attended one of Winston Churchill's meetings to call for his support on women's suffrage. Churchill refused to answer the questions they called out to him, as candidates often did. But when the police were called Christabel realized that she had not done enough to get arrested – and she needed to be arrested to get publicity for the WSPU. She had to somehow assault the police who held her with her arms pinned behind her back – but how on earth could she do that? Knowing it would count as a technical assault, she spat at one of the policeman who held her. The women were arrested and charged, and several of them were sent to prison.

Winston Churchill was alarmed by the imprisonment, and fearful of the effect that might have on his campaign. (At that time Churchill was in favour of some sort of women's suffrage and had even voted in favour of it in 1904, in the House of Commons.) He visited the prison and offered to pay the fines so the women could be released. The women, and the prison governor, both refused to accept his money. And Keir Hardie sent the women a telegram of encouragement, saying that their actions would do their cause immense good.

▦

Sylvia Pankhurst was first imprisoned at the end of 1906, when parliament had reassembled after the long summer break, and the WSPU had organized a protest at Westminster. A small but very noisy crowd of women tried to get inside the parliament building and talk to the MPs. Increasingly exasperated by the women's persistence, angry policeman bundled them roughly out of the lobby and down the steps of the building into Parliament Square. There about ten of the women were arrested, including Sylvia's younger sister, Adela, but not Sylvia herself.

The next day Sylvia went to the court to find out what the women's sentences were, and protested to the magistrate about the treatment of her friends. When she was flung out of the court for her impudence she still wouldn't give up, and tried to make a speech to WSPU supporters on the courthouse steps. The magistrate was so outraged that a young woman dared to question him and challenge the judgement of his court that he had Sylvia arrested as well, on a charge of obstruction. She was sent to Holloway Prison for 14 days.

In the months that followed, the suffragettes' deliberate courting of arrest and imprisonment increased. When they lobbied parliament now, they refused to take no for an answer, and instead made a scene. The WSPU believed that the government itself must legislate in their favour, and they must give it no peace until it did.

The women's actions and their sentences had shocked many British people, in a way that the suffragettes' demands had not moved or shocked them before. The imprisonments were discussed in the House of Commons where Keir Hardie appealed for a reduction in their terms, while other MPs loudly applauded the treatment of what they claimed were *"female hooligans"*.

The *London Evening News* newspaper carried an article by Emmeline Pethick-Lawrence, one of the leaders of the WSPU. It was both a shout of triumph, and a call to arms:

> The struggle has begun. It is a life and death struggle. We appeal to none but women to rise up and fight by our side, shoulder to shoulder... We are not sorry for ourselves – the harder the fight, the better. What we are going to get is a great revolt of the women against their subjection of body and mind to men.

Any respectable gentleman of the professional classes who read that probably thought it a load of nonsense. Women's suffrage had a long way to go before it became accepted as an irresistible force. But those fighting words were prophetic. From that day forward the suffragettes gloried in their dank prison cells and coarse prison clothes – which until then had represented nothing but shame for anyone at any level of society. Thoroughly respectable women, who had never before taken a public stand in opposition to men, turned those shameful symbols into marks of glory and achievement. They turned themselves into martyrs (people who are willing to suffer for a cause), and martyrs are very difficult to defeat.

And the war of the women had only just begun. Now, with increasing pressure from militant suffragettes at every turn, the politicians' war of retaliation upon the women increased as well. Both sides, in fact, began to move steadily up a scale in their levels of response – from exasperation, annoyance and irritation on both sides, towards more savage and violent moves. There is no doubt that the suffragettes' actions aroused intense male hostility. Suffragettes were frequently pummelled by men in the audiences of the meetings they disrupted. Bands of young men, spoiling for a fight, often disrupted suffragette meetings too, especially those held outside London, and the WSPU learned to conceal barbed wire behind the flowers that stood along the front of the speakers' platforms.

Up and down the country, however, more and more women were roused to join the WSPU – gentlewomen and laundry girls, professional women and titled ladies. It was a great unifying wave of feeling, and although the Labour Party still offered a beacon of hope to many, there was now less party allegiance and party activism within the suffrage movement. In all the parties, in fact, women began to desert their previous political commitments and declare their readiness to support any candidate who would take up their cause. What use was a constitutional policy to those who have no constitutional weapon? asked Christabel Pankhurst. They must devise other weapons to use.

Sylvia wrote in detail about her first experience in prison as soon as she was released. She continued to record her experiences each of the many times she was imprisoned. Two things are always clear from what she says. One is how shocking jail was for her; the other is how moved she was by the plight of the ordinary women who were imprisoned in Holloway on charges that had nothing to do with women's suffrage.

Nothing could have prepared Sylvia for Holloway. She had no idea what imprisonment was like, and nor did any of the other middle-class or aristocratic women who now experienced it. To explain this in today's terms you might try to imagine someone from modern Britain who took for granted their high standard of living and their pleasingly civilized life – someone who had never experienced anything else – being transported to a hell-hole prison, in a country where no laws safeguard their treatment.

After her first arrest, Sylvia was taken to Holloway from the Magistrates' Court in a filthy "Black Maria" prison van. She was locked in a tiny dark compartment in the van and surrounded by shrieking women from another court whose voices echoed around her in the inky blackness as the van lurched through the streets. When the Black Maria reached the prison she was locked up for hours in a pitch-dark cubicle, shivering with shock, cold and exhaustion, whilst more batches of prisoners were brought in and locked up as well. Then Sylvia was part of a group of prisoners who were marched barefoot to a medical inspection, and on into a filthy bathroom. *"The baths were indescribably dirty,"* Sylvia wrote later. *"I shuddered at stepping into the water clouded with the scum of previous occupants."*

After the compulsory bath, a female warder gave her some strange shabby garments to put on from a miserable pile of arrow-marked brown clothing, and then screamed at her in indignant scorn because Sylvia hadn't put on any stays. Stays were a kind of corset that most women wore at that time. They were heavy and bulky and laced tightly down the front, and when they were worn correctly they restricted movement as well as breathing. But suffragettes (along with other progressive women of the time) had given up wearing such things when they also gave up skirts that touched the ground, and hat veils to pull down modestly over their faces when they went out in public. After a lot of argument, Sylvia was allowed to leave the stays off.

Finally, many hours after her arrest, Sylvia was locked up alone in a cell just 7 feet by 5 feet (2.1 metres by 1.5

metres) with a stone floor and a tiny barred window near the ceiling. That was only just enough space for a human body to lie down and stretch out, but scarcely more room to move. The cell held a wooden shelf, a mattress and blankets, and a plank bed on the floor. A slop pail for waste water and to use as an emergency lavatory, a thin towel, a can of drinking water, a cup and a plate were the standard equipment.

Sylvia had to learn to live a bewilderingly different life for those first two weeks. She never got used to the conditions, although she returned to them many times – and proper sleep was always impossible. Later, she explained that the cell was so *"cold and stuffy"* she could only doze for a few minutes at a time.

Long before daylight the prisoners were woken by a tremendous clatter as the cell blocks were unlocked and the morning warders began their duties. First the prisoners had to wash and dress, empty their slop pails and roll up their bedding. All this had to be conducted in silence – any noise from any of the prisoners was immediately challenged and punished. Next, the women scrubbed out their cells, which were inspected before a thin gruel and a slice of bread were delivered. If the scrubbing wasn't good enough – and Sylvia's often failed the inspection – then the work had to be repeated until it was approved.

The women all then worked alone in their cells sewing various garments that had been commissioned from the prison by outside companies. (Today prisoners are paid a small amount for any work they do; then, no work was

THE NEW PRIME MINISTER: THE RIGHT HON. H. H. ASQUITH.

Herbert Henry Asquith became leader of the Liberal Party and the Prime Minister in 1908, after the resignation of Sir Henry Campbell-Bannerman.

A cartoon mocking Asquith's opinion on women's right to vote.

Two suffragettes take an opportunity to confront Asquith in the street. Behind him is Sir Edward Grey, a Liberal MP who supported women's suffrage.

Sylvia Pankhurst speaking at her headquarters in the East End of London in October 1912.

Leading members of the Women's Social and Political Union (WSPU). From right to left: Sylvia and her older sister Christabel Pankurst, with Emmeline Pethick-Lawrence, Annie Kenney, and Lady Constance Lytton.

Emmeline Pankhurst, Sylvia's mother and founder of the WSPU. She is wearing the Holloway Badge, a medal awarded to imprisoned suffragettes. The badge, probably designed by Sylvia, shows an arrow in the WSPU colours on a silver portcullis or prison gate.

Imprisoned suffragettes on hunger strike faced the horrors of force-feeding. Liquid food was poured through a tube down the prisoner's throat or nose. This anti-Asquith poster was produced for the 1910 election.

During 1913 and 1914 the "Cat and Mouse Act" allowed the government to temporarily release from prison suffragettes on hunger strike who had become dangerously ill. As soon as their health improved, the women were re-arrested to complete their sentence.

By 1914 Sylvia was so weak from hunger, thirst and sleep strikes that her supporters had to carry her in a chair when she went out. She was determined to starve to death unless Asquith agreed to meet a delegation of East London women.

rewarded.) Each prisoner was given a sheet to hem, or a mailbag to sew, or a man's shirt to make. Later in the morning the prisoners left their cells, and were organized into a single file. Sylvia explained that they had to stay completely silent as they marched to the chapel for a solemn religious service. Afterwards they were marched back to their cells to continue their silent and lonely work.

Another cell inspection was followed by lunch of thin oatmeal porridge. Lunch was followed by more sewing. Supper at 5pm was the same as breakfast, and the cell doors were then shut for the night. Twice in each 24 hours the prisoners had a brief opportunity – harried by the constant shout of *"Make haste! Make haste!"* – to run to a lavatory in the corridor, which had only the semi-privacy of a half door on it: *"like a cowshed,"* Sylvia wrote. At 8pm the lights went out and another cold, sleepless night began.

Twice a week Sylvia, like all the prisoners, was allowed to exercise in a bare courtyard for half an hour, again in complete silence. The lack of privacy, the bad food, the lack of exercise, the solitary confinement and the stuffy cold cells: all these quickly took their toll on the health and well-being of most prisoners, and they all certainly affected Sylvia and the other suffragettes.

The suffragettes who had first been arrested in London had been put into what was called the Second Division, inside Holloway prison. From then on, most suffragettes were also consigned to the Second Division in Holloway, and in other prisons, too. There were three prison divisions. First Division prisoners had certain privileges that were denied to other prisoners – the right to wear their own clothes, for example, and to receive visitors. Prisoners in the Second Division did not usually have such privileges but they were often allowed books to read. Their prison clothes were certainly drab and ill fitting but usually of a reasonable quality, and their food, although plain and boring, was usually edible.

Ordinary prisoners were usually put into the Third Division. The magistrate who first sent Sylvia to prison for protesting in his courtroom, and for making a speech on the steps of the court building, sent her to Holloway Prison's Third Division. He probably did that because he was so angry and offended by her behaviour. It may even have been some sort of administrative mistake – it was certainly unusual for someone of Sylvia's background to be treated like that.

Whatever the reason, the Third Division prison conditions in Holloway were a revelatory experience for Sylvia. Unlike most of her suffragette friends, she saw another side to life, and she witnessed and shared the life of ordinary prisoners, working-class women with no friends who could protest their situation in the outside world; ill-educated and confused women who had no idea of the rights and wrongs of their situation. No lawyers had defended these women before they were sentenced, and no important Members of Parliament or political leaders spoke up in their defence. Some of them had been imprisoned for years, with no apparent hope of release. Between 1905 and 1914, almost 35,000 women were imprisoned in England alone. Some were very young; others were pregnant, destitute, or nursing mothers.

When the Third Division prisoners met in chapel – "*row upon row of careworn faces*" wrote Sylvia compassionately – and listened to the chaplain lecture them harshly about their sins, they bowed their heads and wept with misery. "*I wept with those poor souls,*" Sylvia later wrote.

When the cell door closed on me again, the shrunken forms of frail old grannies with their scant white hair, their shaking hands and piteous withered faces, and the tense white looks and burning eyes of younger women haunted me.

Sylvia met some Second Division suffragette prisoners in Holloway on the first day of her sentence. They wore dark green instead of her own dark-brown uniforms, and carried small loaves of brown bread with them that were left over from their previous supper. Since the Third Division had had no supper at all the night before, one of the suffragettes gave Sylvia half of her loaf. Sylvia was eventually transferred to the First Division, together with some other suffragettes. That meant the women were moved into rooms in a remand hospital wing within

Holloway Prison, and were offered the chance to wear their own clothes, and have food sent in from outside by their friends. But the women indignantly refused both of these concessions.

No First Division prison uniform existed at that time, but some new ones, made of heavy grey wool, were invented for them. And because they refused the privilege of sent-in food the suffragettes were served food from the Second Division, which was a little better than Sylvia's had been in the Third Division. The newly elevated First Division suffragettes did accept one set of privileges – being allowed to write and receive a fortnightly letter, and to have books and newspapers sent in by their friends. Encouraged by this, Sylvia demanded the right to have drawing paper, pen and ink, and pencils. When her friends were allowed to supply them, she set about sketching the prison scenes around her.

From the start the authorities were uncertain about how to handle suffragette prisoners, and their treatment varied enormously. The women were at the mercy of magistrates and judges, most of whom were unsympathetic to the suffragette cause. Once they were imprisoned, the women's treatment varied according to the mood of those who had tried and sentenced them – or according to the effectiveness of the political pressure applied from the outside: on their behalf, or against them.

Being imprisoned is never enjoyable: it is not intended to be, although in modern times most civilized countries treat prisoners with some compassion and humanity. But the treatment of the suffragettes in prison was appalling, and sometimes their conditions, like Sylvia's, were deliberately made especially harsh by the magistrates and judges who committed them to prison. They were often treated like hardened criminals, although they had generally committed only minor breaches of the law, and sometimes had done nothing wrong at all.

This treatment was thought a good way to punish and shock them out of continuing their protests when they returned to the outside world. Sometimes their prison experiences had the effect on the suffragettes that the government wanted. Many imprisoned women were horrified by prison; others were made very ill by the conditions in which they were kept. In general the health and mental well-being of the suffragette women suffered significantly. Some of them became so sick in prison that they never completely recovered.

It is very hard to endure such hardship for your principles, but that is what many suffragettes did. They believed that publicity from their imprisonment would help the cause of women's suffrage. And so it did.

When she was released, Sylvia was determined to expose the appalling life of ordinary women prisoners in the Third Division, and gave dozens of interviews to the newspapers. Those early experiences in Holloway never left her; she fought hard to improve the lives of working women for many years.

At first Emmeline and Christabel Pankhurst tried to stop Sylvia from talking about the conditions inside Holloway. They believed that calling for prison reforms would get in the way of women's suffrage and deflect attention from their main campaign, so they did not want the released prisoners to talk about it. However, Sylvia defied the WSPU ruling on this and, as it happened, news of the conditions in prisons did nothing to distract from the suffrage campaign. (In fact, later on, Emmeline and Christabel were photographed in prison clothes themselves, to publicize their activities.)

The experiences of the imprisoned women touched the imagination of the country in a way that quieter methods had not succeeded in doing. More militant demonstrations in Parliament Square followed, and 20 more women were sent to prison. Then the WSPU appealed for prison volunteers throughout Britain, and the rate of imprisonments increased. Fourteen days in Holloway became the general rule for suffragettes, and it brought them worldwide publicity.

Prime Minister Asquith

Asquith

1908

ASQUITH KEPT A DIARY in which he recorded his impressions of the important events of the day. In the diary he called the suffragettes' imprisonment and their later hunger strikes *"novel and disagreeable"*. Asquith had long described himself as an outright antagonist of women's suffrage, and the increased level of action by the WSPU had certainly done nothing to change his mind. If anything, it had further convinced him that he was right to oppose them.

The idea of changing rational beliefs and reasoned argument through marches and parades, and by fighting policeman and being imprisoned, was simply incomprehensible to Asquith. The more the women marched and shouted, the less his sympathy or his understanding marched with them.

The official response of the government to suffragette protest was still to arrest the perpetrators and imprison them. In that sense, nothing had changed. But then, early in 1908, one important thing did change: Asquith became the Prime Minister.

Sir Henry Campbell-Bannerman had four heart attacks during 1907, and began the New Year as a very sick man. In February the King, Edward VII, was about to depart for the south of France for a winter holiday, and called Asquith in to see him. King Edward made it clear that if Campbell-Bannerman had to resign, then Asquith would be asked to head the Liberal government in his place.

For the next few weeks Asquith acted as the Prime Minister in everything but name, and eventually Sir Henry had to accept that he couldn't go on. At the beginning of April he wrote to the King who was still in Biarritz, in the south of France, formally offering his resignation. The next day a royal messenger was dispatched to London, to summon Asquith to a meeting with the King.

Asquith wrote to his wife, Margot, from Biarritz, elated with success. His ambitions had finally been realized, and it was a triumphant moment for him:

This morning I put on a frock coat ... and went to the King who was similarly attired. I presented him with my written resignation of the office of Chancellor of the Exchequer; and he then said "I appoint you Prime Minister and First Lord of the Treasury" whereupon I knelt down and kissed his hand.

Sir Henry Campbell-Bannerman died two weeks later.

Asquith had been dangerous enough to the suffragettes as a member of Campbell-Bannerman's Cabinet. How much more dangerous would he be now that he was in command? Asquith had, if anything, toughened his stand against the women's demands. Yet as a result of the rough handling of the suffragettes, public sympathy for them had begun to grow. The new Prime Minister had to look for new ways to deflect that sympathy.

Asquith's priorities as Prime Minister did not include paying attention to the suffragettes. His main political aims lay in very different directions, and under his leadership the Liberals produced an advanced program of social welfare reforms, including old-age pensions and unemployment insurance. But the suffragettes had no intention of allowing him a period of grace. Not only did their attacks on Asquith himself increase, their scope also widened to include members of his family.

Margot Asquith was spat on by one of the other women guests at the Lord Mayor's Banquet that November, and her own outspoken opposition to female suffrage meant that she was regarded as a traitor both to her own sex and to the cause. She was sent hate mail, some of which contained threats to her children as well as to herself. One night she was woken in Downing Street by the sound of breaking glass, as suffragettes threw stones into the room just below the one in which her young son was sleeping. She accused them of making her life "*a hell*". Defending the treatment suffragettes received in prison, Margot wrote:

Why should my life be burdened by these wombless, vicious, cruel women? They say men would not be so seriously dealt with. What lies they tell! Men would be horsewhipped at every street corner.

The cause of women's suffrage still divided opinion in the House of Commons, and troubled the Liberal Party. But surprisingly, the issue was still of minor importance to most Liberal Party politicians – when they could ignore it, they happily did so. MPs were certainly rattled by the suffragette activities, and the government even announced that no women were to be admitted to a political meeting at which a member of Asquith's Cabinet was to speak. But Asquith focussed his government's attention on the demands of the Royal Navy for more money, on the problem of Home Rule for Ireland, and on trying to restrain the Conservative Party's domination of the House of Lords. He would try to ignore or deflect the women for a while longer.

So the new militancy had been successful in attracting public attention to the women's goals, but not yet in convincing Asquith's government. Asquith and his supporters were generally more politically shrewd than the suffragettes were, which wasn't surprising. The politicians had almost everything on their side: parliamentary power, years of experience, and the use of the police force. They also thought that even if public opinion sympathized with the women, most official opinion, including that of many magistrates and judges, was behind them. And it was.

In the days before radio or television, media influence lay with powerful local and national newspapers. So the government – as well as the suffragettes – had only the printed word by which to attempt to sway public opinion. This did not always go in the government's favour. But although many newspapers expressed outrage at how the protesting women were treated, they didn't often support their cause. The newspapers simply took advantage of the excellent story opportunities the protesters provided.

When a Liberal MP introduced another women's suffrage bill in November 1908, this one called the Women's Enfranchisement Bill, it was voted a second reading (a stage that every bill had to pass before it could become law). But there wasn't enough time for the bill to go through all the necessary stages, unless the government agreed to allow it some extra time. Asquith received a delegation of 60 Liberal MPs, who argued that the Liberal Party must support this bill. But Asquith, who disagreed, was ready for them.

The widening of the franchise – at least to include more men – was a significant item on the Liberal Party's political agenda. Now Asquith told the delegation that he couldn't allow more time for the Women's Enfranchisement Bill because he had better things in mind. He said his government had a *"binding obligation"* to introduce a far-reaching reform bill before the current session of parliament came to an end. That reform bill wouldn't include women, it was true – but Asquith assured MPs that there would be an opportunity for women's suffrage to be added to such a reform bill. And as long as the amendment was drafted on objective lines, Asquith promised that his government would allow an entirely free vote on it, in the House of Commons. (A free vote meant that the government would not tell individual Liberal MPs how to vote – they could vote according to their own consciences.)

Asquith's delaying tactic worked on the Liberal politicians. But the WSPU did not believe his promise. They had heard too many evasions and delaying tactics from him before. They had no intention of waiting any longer if they could find an alternative way forward. And they did not believe that Asquith's *"binding obligation"* reform bill would be amended to include women.

But Asquith held a trump card. As a successful Prime Minister he commanded the loyalty of the Liberal Party, and that loyal support would not desert him in the present conditions. Liberal and Labour MPs alike were more concerned with the matters they thought significant, than with what they saw as the relatively petty grievances of a million comfortably-off women – the women behind the suffrage groups. To such MPs the social conditions of Britain – unemployment, desolate poverty, slum housing – were so appalling that social reform simply had to take priority.

Asquith regarded the militant suffragettes as criminals who deserved punishment. (For that matter, he also believed that the *non*-militant suffragettes were wrong, and lacked a *"soundness of judgement"* in what he saw as their "*unnatural demands*".) Many other Liberal Party politicians were increasingly antagonized by militant action. They thought it an outrage against decent behaviour and believed that the women who were imprisoned deserved every second of their sentences. (If they had a chance directly to influence the magistrates and judges who imposed the sentences or the prison governors who administered them, they probably would have encouraged longer and harsher prison sentences for suffragettes.) Very few MPs spoke out against the imprisonment of suffragettes – only men like Keir Hardie and some other Labour Party MPs publicly sympathized with either the women's cause or with their bravery.

And for all his political delays and concealments, for all that his opponents criticized his motives and strategy in dealing with the suffrage movement, Asquith was still the Prime Minister. What's more, he was the head of a great reforming government, and he was about to embark on an historic showdown with the House of Lords. This "upper" House of Parliament was filled with members of the aristocracy, who took their places in the House of Lords through heredity and not through election. A large majority of them supported the Conservative Party, and objected to the Liberal Party's attempts to redistribute wealth. The House of Lords had the power to block legislation: Asquith's government wanted to take that power away from them. The battle lines were drawn, and Asquith did not intend to be deflected.

Pankhurst

The Hunger Strikes

1909

As PROTESTING WOMEN continued to be arrested and imprisoned, so the publicity for women's suffrage increased. Not all of it was sympathetic, of course, but to the women of the WSPU the publicity itself was the point. They continued to believe that the more their actions drew attention to their cause, the more likely it was that politicians would give in to pressure.

Some women, in protest at the conditions in which they were held, or in protest against their very imprisonment, began to go on hunger strike while they were in prison. Sylvia Pankhurst was one of those women. The hunger strikers refused all food, and sometimes later also refused water in an additional thirst strike, in an effort to increase public attention. They believed that if their hunger strikes were effective, the prison authorities would have no alternative but to let them out of prison early.

Some people can go with very little food for days at a time without becoming ill. If you don't eat at all you will quickly become weak, confused and light-headed, you will certainly prevent your body from performing well, and may do yourself permanent harm. But it is sometimes possible to survive for weeks without any food, and humans may not necessarily suffer permanent damage from that deprivation.

Going without water is a different matter, and a very dangerous one. Dehydration can cause a wide variety of unpleasant symptoms very quickly – like headaches, intense tiredness, muscle and stomach cramps, constipation, and nausea. Water makes up about 70 per cent of human bodies, which shows just what an important part it plays in our health and well-being. When a human body gets low on fluid, almost no essential bodily processes can run at full capacity. Without water, your body quickly starts to close down.

At first, people who go without water feel their mouths and throats to be unbearably swollen and dry. Sylvia Pankhurst went on thirst strikes several times to try to speed up her prison sentences. She wrote:

There was always a horrible taste in the mouth which grows more parched as the days pass with the tongue dry and hot and thickly coated. The saliva comes thick and yellow; a bitter tasting phlegm rises constantly so nasty that one retches violently but is denied the relief of sickness. The urine, growing thicker, darker, more scanty, is passed with difficulty. There is no action of the bowels during imprisonment.

On a hunger and thirst strike, Sylvia sometimes permitted herself what she called a *"great luxury"* – rinsing out her mouth with water once a day. She never did that more than once a day in case her tongue absorbed moisture, and she was careful *"never to swallow a single drop"*. She added: *"I was always cold, but I felt only a trace of hunger, and less as the days passed. Thirst strikers crave only for water."*

If someone persists with a thirst strike they will probably soon faint or lose consciousness. If they persist for long, much worse will happen. Their livers will start to malfunction, and be unable to expel toxins from the body. If they persist in not drinking anything at all, even for a relatively short period of time, they will die. That is why the suffragettes thought combined hunger and thirst strikes were their trump card: they would *have* to be let out of prison, for the authorities would not want them to die in prison in such circumstances.

An artist friend of Sylvia's called Marion Wallace Dunlop began the first suffragette hunger strike in the summer of 1909. She was arrested for writing words of protest on the stone walls near the Houses of Parliament, and was imprisoned for a month. As soon as she entered Holloway Prison she demanded to be treated as a political prisoner, which the governor refused. Marion then told the prison governor that she would fast until her demands were met.

The prison authorities were alarmed. They tried every means they could devise to coax her into eating, even leaving a tray of delicious food (not the sort normally available in prison) in her cell all night. The governor assured her that the Home Secretary would ignore her and that she would be left to die, but her cheerful courage continued. *"What will you have today?"* the doctors and female warders asked anxiously at breakfast-time. *"My determination,"* answered Marion cheerfully. Her fast lasted for 90 hours – and then, without warning or comment, she was released triumphant.

From then on, hunger strikes became an obstinate problem for the authorities, and a successful method of newsworthy protest for the suffragettes. Marion Wallace-Dunlop's release was greeted with joy and intense relief from those who knew of her ordeal. She had staked her life on the reluctance of the government to let a woman die in prison, and dozens of women were inspired by her example and willing to follow it.

The WSPU leaders had not ordered or authorized the hunger strike, but they recognized a brilliant public relations opportunity when they saw one, and embraced the idea wholeheartedly. When 14 more women were arrested soon after Marion was released, they too refused food until they were granted political status. They refused to change into prison clothes, and although they were then stripped naked by the female warders in an attempt to force them into submission, their determination held.

Throughout the summer of 1909, suffragettes continued to regain their freedom soon after being imprisoned, by hunger striking. When women in Holloway began this protest the outside world was horrified – and the government was dismayed.

By the autumn of 1909, 37 imprisoned suffragette women had successfully managed to terminate their prison sentences by going on hunger strikes. (Four of the women had even managed to do that twice in succession.) Thousands more women added their own courage and determination, and now the hunger strikers pushed the boundaries of the volatile mixture even further out. Could the women win despite the politicians' opposition? They believed that they could.

Mass gatherings continued to be organized and more women were arrested; by-election candidates were still pestered by suffragettes; but still, there were signs that the suffragette novelty was wearing thin. The danger now was that the WSPU might seem stale – that its activities would produce nothing fresh to seize the public imagination or sustain the attention of the media. So the strategies of the suffragettes grew ever more daring, especially in attending political meetings where they could speak out and disrupt the meeting or provoke enough antagonism to attract attention. The official exclusion of women from such meetings simply encouraged them to try more daring ways to flout the ban.

When Winston Churchill was due to speak in Dundee in October, for example, Isabel Kelley climbed scaffolding outside the hall and lowered herself on a rope on to the roof of the hall. There she lay concealed for 17 hours until the meeting began, when she let herself down through a skylight and rushed into the hall to protest. Other suffragettes had been smuggled into the meeting to support her cries of "*Votes for women!*" and to pick up the challenge of disruption one after another, as each woman was grabbed, silenced, and hustled out of the hall.

Just at this time, however, the actions of Asquith's government imposed even more suffering on those suffragettes willing to be imprisoned for their cause. Ironically, these actions also brought the suffragettes a fresh wave of public sympathy.

Punishing Mary Leigh

THE *DAILY NEWS* APPEALED to Emmeline Pankhurst to check what it called *"disgraceful developments"*, but the WSPU continued to develop its anti-government protests. Another determined woman in Liverpool, Mary Leigh, climbed up to the roof of a building opposite the hall in which Richard Haldane – a member of the Liberal Cabinet and a known anti-suffragist – was speaking. She stood there amongst the chimney-stacks throwing slates on to the roof of the hall, while her suffragette comrades in the street below shouted encouragement and suffrage slogans through a megaphone.

A few months later Mary Leigh repeated this tactic in Birmingham, when Asquith spoke at a meeting at Bingley Hall. Together with another suffragette called Charlotte Marsh, Mary stood on a nearby roof and ripped up slates, which they flung on to the roof of the hall. Fire hoses were turned on them, but the two women simply took off their shoes so they wouldn't slip on the wet roof, and continued throwing the slates until Asquith left.

On another occasion Mary Leigh rushed the carriage in which the Prime Minister was riding, and tossed a small hatchet into it. Eight other women were arrested for window breaking, and one for throwing an iron bar through the window of a carriage of the train in which Asquith was returning to London.

Asquith and his colleagues must have found the increased levels of violent protest extremely alarming: any one would. Being constantly attacked and challenged in such personal ways is very hard to endure with dignity or confidence. Asquith's natural inclination was to continue to ignore the protests, but at the same time he knew that the suffragettes were attracting both attention and sympathy around the country. The women were flouting the law by forcing prisons to release them before their sentences were completed. They were making a mockery of the courts. They had to be stopped – but how?

When Mary Leigh was arrested after the Liverpool incident she was sent to prison, where she immediately went on hunger strike. By then, Asquith's government was infuriated and exasperated with the whole situation. The Cabinet was in no mood to seem to be made fools of by a group of wild women. They were determined to stop them with a new policy, which they hoped would defeat the suffragettes' prison tactics. They decided that

Mary Leigh would be a good suffragette to try this out on – she was young and healthy and her protests had been particularly offensive. So Mary's prison governor was instructed to ensure that Mary Leigh ate. If she refused food, and if she continued to refuse it – well then, she must be forcibly fed.

Force-feeding is very unpleasant. It is also very unpleasant to read about – though reading about it is not, of course, as bad as enduring it. But if you easily feel disgusted or nauseous reading descriptions of such things you had better brace yourself before you read on, or skip the next few pages.

Force-feeding was quite often used in the 1800s and early 1900s, in what were then called lunatic asylums. (Now we call such places mental hospitals, and treat the patients in them with more compassion and understanding.) Force-feeding is not common today, or at least not in its original form. If patients today cannot – or will not – feed themselves, then nourishing liquids (or even just a saline solution to keep their bodies topped up with essential fluids) can be given to them through a tube that is attached to a vein, called an intravenous drip. The patients' bodies absorb the liquid, and so their life can be sustained. That technique is often used for medical reasons in modern hospitals after serious surgery and it has sometimes been used in recent times on hunger strikers.

But in 1909 medical science was not so advanced, and intravenous drips had not been invented. At that time, force-feeding involved pushing a tube into a patient's mouth and down the back of their throat into their gullet. Then some sort of liquid food could be poured or even pumped down the tube, and so into the patient's stomach. If the patient tried to resist by clamping their teeth shut, a metal brace could be inserted into their mouth and wound open, slowly forcing their jaws apart. And if the patient resisted the treatment by trying to bite the tube or cough it up, then force-feeding could still be achieved by pushing the tube down their nose instead of their throat.

The dangerous effects of force-feeding were well known to doctors because of the experience of trying it in mental hospitals, and sometimes in prison hospitals with other protesters. Several leading medical experts were appalled that such a method was used on suffragette women, and they protested about it in newspapers and through sympathetic MPs. One medical expert, Dr Anderson Moxley, was accustomed to treating patients in mental hospitals who refused food. He explained that he had long since given up using a pump in force-feeding because it risked injury to heart and lungs, and even risked killing the patient if they had any heart disease. One obvious danger was that the liquid food would be forced into the patient's lungs instead of down the throat – and that did happen several times to suffragettes.

Dr Moxley reported a case in which the patient's tongue had become twisted behind the tube and partially torn off. He also claimed that force-feeding *"injured the* constitution and lacerated the mouth, and broke or ruined the teeth". In normal people, he continued, the effect would also be to "injure the digestive organs, and aggravate any bronchial condition which may exist, and to cause dangerous chronic symptoms". Other doctors joined the protest, claiming that some of its victims would be driven insane by such inhuman treatment. And Dr Forbes Ross declared in the Observer newspaper that:

> ...as a medical man without any particular feeling for the cause of the Suffragettes, I consider forcible feeding by the methods employed an act of brutality beyond common endurance.

When news of forcible feeding was made public it produced horror and outrage in the British public. It is easy to see why – the subject is a gruesome one, and the suffragettes' reports of the treatment certainly did not avoid the most disgusting details of their experiences. Keir Hardie accused Asquith's government of committing an outrageous crime against women, and spoke out passionately in the House of Commons.

> *Women, worn and weak with hunger are seized upon, held down by brute force, gagged, a tube inserted down the throat, and food poured or pumped into the stomach. Let British men think over the spectacle.*

Two journalists resigned their jobs on the *Daily News*, a Liberal paper, because of the Liberal government's actions. At that time, reports of torture by the Czar's government in Russia were being roundly condemned in the paper. The journalists wrote a joint protest letter to *The Times* that said: *"We cannot denounce torture in Russia and support it in England."*

The government and its supporters tried to argue that it was *"wicked folly"* for the women to try to starve themselves to death in the first place, but that did not satisfactorily counter the descriptions of forcible feeding. Churchill blustered to a deputation from the NUWSS at this time that their cause *"had marched backwards"* because of the militant suffragettes' actions, but that seems more like wishful thinking than reality – the suffragettes had gained immense public sympathy. Asquith himself was closer to the truth of the day when, in his memoirs, he admitted that force-feeding had been *"repugnant"*.

Being Force-Fed

FROM 1909 ONWARDS, Sylvia Pankhurst was force-fed many times during her imprisonments, and she described the usual procedure in her books. Six female warders entered her cell and flung her on her back, holding her down firmly by shoulders and wrists, hips, knees and ankles. Then the doctors arrived, and tried to force open her mouth, but Sylvia kept it tightly closed.

She later wrote about what happened next.

A steel instrument pressed my gums, cutting into the flesh. I braced myself to receive that terrible pain ... I wrenched my head free. Again they grasped me. Again the struggle. Again the steel cutting its way in, though I strained my force against it. Then something gradually forced my jaws apart as the screw was turned; the pain was like having teeth drawn. They were trying to get the tube down my throat. I was struggling madly to stiffen my muscles and close my throat. They got it down I suppose though I was unconscious of anything then save a mad revolt of struggling, for they said at last 'That's all' and I vomited as the tube came up. They left me on the bed exhausted, gasping for breath and sobbing convulsively.

Morning and evening, day after day, Sylvia endured the same agony. Her gums were always sore and bleeding with ragged bits of flesh hanging from them.

Because suffragettes were likely to try to resist, the preferred method of force-feeding them was to push a narrow tube up the women's noses rather than down their throats. Usually each woman would be held down by female warders or nurses, or strapped tightly into a chair, while the tube was inserted and the liquid poured or pumped down it.

Many women found the barbaric procedure appallingly painful, as well as humiliating. Some suffragettes fainted when they were force-fed; others, like Sylvia, vomited up the liquid food immediately after the procedure had ended and so they had often to go through it all again, immediately.

Forcible feeding was not used on all of the suffragette prisoners who refused food. The prison authorities tended to pick and choose their victims from amongst the young and healthy, no doubt because of the known dangers of the procedure.

Sylvia wrote that the fear of being force-fed – the agony of waiting for the arrival of the warders and the doctors – was almost as painful as the process itself. She described how she felt after a doctor had examined her in her cell and pronounced her fit for force-feeding. Sylvia was thrown into an agitated misery as she waited. Her heart raced; her head rang with noises; cold shivers ran down her spine. Resolving to fight – though knowing she was helpless – she gathered everything in her cell that might be used as a missile: the prison mug and plate, her outdoor shoes – and stood with them against the back wall of the cell, waiting to hurl them at the doctors when they returned. She wrote:

> *Presently I heard footsteps approaching. I was strangled with fear, cold and stunned, yet alert to every sound. The door opened – not the doctors but a crowd of wardresses filled the doorway.*

Sylvia couldn't bring herself to throw her missiles at the female warders, for she regarded the women as simply the tools of the doctors. She struggled with the women empty-handed, but they overcame her.

Sylvia had to endure force-feeding because she was judged strong enough to withstand its effects, but her mother, Emmeline, was only threatened with it. Doctors and female warders came to Emmeline Pankhurst's cell to carry it out, but after she made determined protests against the treatment they went away and she was not force-fed after all, then or later.

The prison authorities also tended to avoid force-feeding any prisoner who was well known in society, especially any aristocratic *"ladies of rank"* – like Lady Constance Lytton, for example. Lady Constance had been arrested several times for her women's suffrage activities, but had been quickly released when the authorities had realized who she was and how fragile her health was. Determined to share in the sufferings of other suffragettes, however, Lady Constance disguised herself as a seamstress and addressed a meeting of people outside Walton Gaol in Liverpool, where hunger striking and force-feeding were at their height. When she was arrested she gave her name as Jane Warton, and was sentenced to 14 days' hard labour.

Lady Constance immediately began a hunger strike and within a day the force-feeding began, despite her poor health that must have been obvious to the doctors. A few days later the suspicions of the authorities were aroused and Lady Constance was released soon afterwards. But the force-feeding had already had its effects, and a series of heart attacks and seizures followed. Lady Constance remained partly paralysed for the rest of her life. The publicity her experiences received revealed the harsh methods by which Asquith's government was trying to break the suffragettes' resistance.

Broken Promises

IN THE SPRING OF 1910 Asquith called an election to try to strengthen his hand in his battle to reform the House of Lords. He knew that if the Liberal Party was returned with another big majority he would be able to push home his reforms more easily. Of course, Asquith also knew he would constantly be questioned about votes for women during the election campaign. He had a strategy ready for that.

During the campaign, Asquith renewed an earlier pledge that he had made, which seemed to offer a way forward on women's suffrage. He said that if his government was re-elected – and so could follow its plan to introduce a reform bill – it would allow a free vote on any amendment to that bill that gave votes to women.

That offer seemed full of hopeful possibilities. In these circumstances, and believing what Asquith said, the exhausted and embattled WSPU offered a truce. They would suspend all the militant tactics of their members.

However, the election did not go Asquith's way. Instead of retaining their large parliamentary majority (or increasing it, as Asquith had hoped), the Liberals lost 100 seats. Now the Liberals had only two more seats in the House of Commons than the Conservative Party. To stay in power, the Liberals had to come to an agreement with other parties in parliament, or they could easily be defeated in any House of Commons vote. So Asquith's government was now completely dependent on the voting support of the Labour Party and the Irish Nationalists in the battle with the House of Lords – and would always have Conservative MPs breathing down their necks.

Most Labour Party MPs were sympathetic to the cause of women's suffrage, but now they were pledged to support the Liberal Party. They did not want to jeopardize the Liberals' fight against the House of Lords. And until they achieved their goal of Home Rule for Ireland, the Irish Nationalists would do anything to keep a Liberal government in power: they saw the Liberal Party as their only hope of success. So once again it seemed that women's suffrage would probably be submerged by other concerns.

Nevertheless, an all-party group of MPs got together and formed a Conciliation Committee. They were determined to try to draft out a suffrage compromise, something that would end the suffragettes' protests and yet not alarm the anti-suffrage politicians.

The compromise legislation they came up with would give votes to women householders, and to other women who occupied business premises with a high rateable value. That would enfranchise only about one million women – mostly the elderly and spinsters. It would do almost nothing for young working women or married women, and would leave about seven million women still unable to vote.

Most suffrage organizations supported this move, as well as most newspapers. To many people, it seemed that such a compromise was the only possible way forward. Could it get the support of the House of Commons? And if it did, would the Lords agree? The Conciliation Committee thought so.

The debate in parliament lasted for two days, which reflected the true depth of feeling on the matter. But Asquith was not prepared to allow even this restricted measure to move forward into law. He and two other important Liberal politicians – Winston Churchill and David Lloyd George – voted against it just before parliament went into its summer recess.

Asquith said in the House of Commons that if the cause of women's suffrage had not won its way to public acceptance by persuasion, argument, organization and peaceful agitation, then it *"had already pronounced its own sentence of death"*. He, for one, was not going to support it. And with the Prime Minister's opposition still so strong, the chances of success for the suffragettes receded still further.

And when parliament returned that autumn after its long break, Asquith announced he would dissolve parliament again and hold yet *another* general election on the issue of the House of Lords. He believed he could get a better result for his Liberal Party this time around. In these circumstances, there would be no more time for the Conciliation Bill before the election. Asquith told a friend that it was *"a great relief that the women have been bowled over for this session."*

Black Friday

ANY ATTEMPT BY PARLIAMENT or the government at compromise also seemed be have been bowled over. The women saw the Conciliation Bill's delays and diversions as a mockery, intended to exasperate and taunt them. Many activists were genuinely confused by this series of setbacks. What on earth could they do next? Even non-militant suffragists like Millicent Fawcett were dismayed at this turn of events. She even appealed to Liberal ministers for guidance on how women might find a peaceful solution to their problem.

The decision to dissolve parliament and hold another election was announced on 18 November 1910. The suffrage groups had been warned of the likelihood of this, and had organized their joint plans for that day accordingly. Emmeline Pankhurst of the WSPU and Elizabeth Garrett Anderson of the NUWSS led a deputation to the House of Commons, hoping to see the Prime Minister and persuade him to withdraw his veto on the Conciliation Bill. They were received politely inside the parliament buildings – but outside in Parliament Square the suffragettes who followed them were treated so violently that the day was known as *"Black Friday"*. The police were sick of controlling crowds of self-righteous women, and it seemed as though their instructions on dealing with them had been changed.

The WSPU had appointed Sylvia to observe the demonstration rather than participate in it. She watched appalled as women were repeatedly battered, struck and flung to the ground. Nothing like this sort of violence had been seen before. Policemen grabbed elderly women by their breasts or hair; young girls were punched and kicked. Fifty women were seriously injured and two died as a result of those injuries. But when those women who had been arrested appeared in court the next day most of the charges were withdrawn; the government wanted to seem magnanimous on the eve of another election.

Five days later Asquith made a statement on women's suffrage. He said that if his government was still in power after the election, he would proceed with a franchise reform bill as long as it could be freely amended. This time, few women believed him – there were too many loopholes for the Liberals to slip through.

But there seemed to be no alternative than to continue to try to push the Liberal government towards legislation. What else could the women do? How else could they achieve what they wanted? If Asquith and his government thought they would just give up and go away – well, they could only try to show him he was wrong.

▦

During the election campaign the activities of the suffragettes continued much as before. There were the usual attempts to challenge members of the Liberal Party Cabinet, and Asquith came in for repeated attacks. In one daring feat a suffragette managed to jump on the running board of Asquith's motor car when he was travelling to an election meeting in St Andrews in Scotland. The woman described what happened next, before the police pulled her away and arrested her. "*We gazed at each other,*" she said. "*I a little dazed at having succeeded so easily: he leaning back in his car, looking white and frightened rather like a fascinated rabbit.*" Asquith was probably worried that she would rip off his clothes, as two other suffragettes had just tried to do at the Lossiemouth golf course. And when he won his election in East Fife, Asquith was prevented from delivering his acceptance speech by suffragettes who climbed up the lamp posts and shouted "*Votes for women!*" so loudly that nothing else – and no one else – could possibly be heard.

The election again left the Liberals and Conservatives almost neck and neck in parliament, so the Liberal government was still dependent on Irish Nationalist and

Labour Party votes. Nevertheless, three MPs who had been successful in the ballot for private members' bills got together and prepared to reintroduce a modified version of the old Conciliation Bill.

Sylvia Pankhurst was still scornful of this bill. She pointed out that now, in its modified form, it was even less helpful to women than before: it would give the vote only to women householders. (The other women originally included had been thrown out in an effort to get more support from other groups in the House of Commons.) Getting the vote was very important to working-class women, as Sylvia had learned from women like Annie Kenney, and from the political work she had started to do in the East End of London. To working women the right to vote wasn't just something to put them on equal terms with men. They wanted to use it for the same purpose as working men did – to give them better working conditions. Sylvia declared:

> *Every woman in England longs for political freedom to make the lot of workers pleasanter, and to bring about reforms. They do not want it as a plaything.*

So the Conciliation Committee's idea of giving the vote to such a narrow section of British women, and ignoring the needs of working women, appalled Sylvia. But most of the suffrage societies were so desperate for results – for any results at all – that they welcomed the bill with enthusiasm. And when the Conciliation Bill passed for a second reading in the House of Commons by the massive majority of 255 votes to 88, they were very encouraged. Now they concentrated on pressing the Liberal government to give it enough time for discussion. If that time were not allocated, the bill would fail.

▦

Once again, however, the women's hopes were dashed. Two weeks later Asquith's government told the House of Commons that they would not, after all, allow time for the Conciliation Bill in this session of parliament. It could have a week in the next session: that was all. But the Conciliation Bill's supporters knew a week would not be long enough. What if its opponents got together again as they had in similar situations in the past, and talked the bill out? What if this was just another delaying trick?

It was an agonizing decision. King Edward VII had died, and a new King, George V, was to be crowned. None of the suffrage organizations wanted to continue a militant campaign throughout the coronation celebrations. But could they justify suspending it?

Sir Edward Grey, a member of Asquith's Cabinet and a supporter of women's suffrage, offered reassurance to the NUWSS and the WSPU representatives. He said the government's offer was not a bogus one, and opponents of suffrage would not be permitted to obstruct or wreck the Conciliation Bill when it returned. And what if a week to debate the bill turned out not to be long enough?

Well then, Sir Edward said, if parliament voted to carry on for longer, the government would not oppose it. It all sounded fair enough, and Sir Edward was known to be an honest man. Christabel Pankhurst admitted: *"We were glad to be able to justify to ourselves a non-militant policy."* Militant action was suspended.

Asquith
Truce
1911

IN 1911 ASQUITH finally achieved success in his battle with the House of Lords, which had steadily opposed almost all his reforms since the Liberal government had taken power in 1906. The Lords could no longer block "money bills" that came from the Commons, and were restricted in the right to delay other legislation. That opened the way for Home Rule for Ireland – a measure that the House of Lords had long opposed.

The Irish Nationalists scented victory for their cause. They were determined to seize their advantage and keep the Liberal Party in power whatever the cost. Any sympathy they may have had for the suffragettes evaporated, especially because of a rumour that Asquith would resign if women's suffrage were introduced against his will. (Without Asquith, the Irish Nationalists knew they would not achieve Home Rule.) Asquith's public anti-suffragism had been so uncompromising that his position was bound to be undermined if his government had to pass any suffrage reform, and many Liberals also feared the issue would break the government. So the Prime Minister was still assured of a majority for his tough line on suffrage.

The way was also clear for the widening of the franchise for men, which the government had promised years earlier. Now Asquith said that his government would introduce a franchise reform bill the following year. He added that, although he was personally opposed to including women in the bill, he would leave MPs in the House of Commons free to make that amendment if they wanted to.

Was that just a trick to defeat the Conciliation Bill? Asquith assured a women's suffrage delegation that it was not a trick. He said that if the Commons voted in favour of an amendment the government would accept that and give it the time it needed.

Could Asquith and his Cabinet be trusted or believed? Many women wanted to trust him. They dreaded a return to militant action. They were convinced that they could win support from enough MPs to add the necessary women's amendments to the promised franchise reform bill. And they believed that they could still keep the Conciliation Bill as a fallback. But they simply did not know if they could really trust the government.

The events of the past few years, and especially the recent majorities in the House of Commons that had voted for some sort of women's suffrage law, filled the women's movement with hope. But Asquith's determination to block women's suffrage did not falter.

Any future for a Conciliation Bill, despite its success in the House of Commons, was doubtful. A majority vote in favour of the bill on a first or second reading was a good start. But Asquith's government knew there was still a clear division of feeling in parliament about women's suffrage. They believed that division was reflected throughout the country. So the government felt justified in refusing to give any more time to the bill.

In a later vote, the House of Commons agreed to send the Conciliation Bill to a committee of the whole House of Commons, where nothing was decided. This meant that no real progress was ever possible with the bill. (In fact, the final revised version of the Conciliation Bill was defeated – by only 14 votes – in November 1912.)

The Storm Rages

THE WSPU DECIDED it could not, did not, and *would* not trust the Liberal Party's latest promises. The call to militancy went out across the country once again, and once again ordinary women answered it with enthusiasm. Money poured in to the organization's funds, and a new technique for public disruption was developed. Suffragettes were tired of the physical battering they received at demonstrations and protests. Now they decided to turn to window-breaking and similar public disorder as a way of getting arrested without having first to endure assault and injury.

Years later Sylvia Pankhurst admitted that she hadn't been sure that increased militancy was what the suffrage movement needed at that stage. Sylvia believed that a stronger appeal to ordinary working women would have been more effective, and certainly seemed to her more necessary. But she added, "*I would rather have died at the stake than say one word against the actions of those who were in the throes of the fight.*" And that attitude reflected the view of many of the suffragette women. They often saw themselves as an isolated and besieged band of fighters whose only hope of success was to stick together – shoulder to shoulder – against the opposition.

Sylvia wrote about how the new militant campaign was organized:

> *Motors were driven at dusk to quiet country lanes, where flints [stones] could be obtained. Would-be window-breakers met Marion Wallace Dunlop or some other trusted member of the WSPU at somebody's flat, and were furnished with hammers or black bags filled with flints.*

The women then made their way by taxi or public transport to their chosen target, jumped out and threw their stones before anyone could stop them. Some of the women were arrested but many others succeeded in making a quick get-away. Many government buildings were attacked, and the windows of the National Liberal Club were broken.

Soon, more extreme activities began to creep in. One suffragette called Emily Wilding Davison was arrested when she threw a lighted paraffin-soaked rag into a post box. Someone else threw a case through the window of Lloyd George's car (Lloyd George was then Chancellor of the Exchequer) and bruised his cheek. When Asquith returned to London from Scotland, a hostile party of suffragettes met his train. Only the Prime Minister's bodyguards were able to keep them from attacking him – although his daughter Violet also managed to get in a blow for her father by *"crunching the fingers of one of the hussies"* as Asquith later described it.

The King's Speech at the opening of the new session of parliament did include a suffrage reform bill that would give the vote to all men over the age of 21. But it contained no mention of women.

It isn't surprising that the suffrage groups were thrown into a new turmoil of suspicion. They had already decided not to trust the Liberals – but they were disappointed to be proved right!

Emmeline Pankhurst told a dinner for released suffragette prisoners that *"the argument of the broken window pane"* was the most valuable one in modern politics. *"It is the argument I am going to use,"* she declared. And, infuriated by a Cabinet member telling an anti-suffrage meeting that there had as yet been no great outburst of public feeling for the suffragettes, the WSPU responded with a positive orgy of stone-throwing. They would give the doubting Cabinet a display of public feeling!

Sylvia was about to leave for a fund-raising trip to America so she did not join in the activities for long – but she reported them with relish in her books:

*In Piccadilly, Regent Street, Oxford Street, Bond Street,
Coventry Street and their neighbourhood, in Whitehall,
Parliament, Trafalgar Square, Cockspur Street and the
Strand as well as in districts as far away as Chelsea,
well-dressed women suddenly produced strong
hammers from innocent looking bags and parcels and
fell on shop windows. Damage amounting to thousands
of pounds was effected in a few moments.*

Meantime Emmeline Pankhurst took a cab to Downing Street and broke windows at Number Ten before she was arrested. Along with 218 other women, she was sent to prison for two months.

The destruction was deliberately intended to cause as much damage as possible, in the hope that insurance companies would add their voice to the pressure on the government. It was not surprising that the government responded savagely once property was damaged on a large scale. In March a warrant was issued for the arrest of three leading members of the WSPU: Christabel Pankhurst, Emmeline Pethick-Lawrence, and her husband Frederick. Together with Emmeline Pankhurst (who was still in prison) they were to stand trial for conspiracy to incite malicious property damage – a very serious offence.

Christabel managed to elude the police and fled to Paris, which caused a fresh uproar in parliament. The Pethick-Lawrences were arrested and charged, together with Emmeline Pankhurst. Outraged shopkeepers demanded compensation from the WSPU for the window-breaking episodes, the insurance companies put pressure on the government, and tempers throughout the country were running high.

Sylvia returned from the fund-raising trip to America, appalled at the danger that faced her mother and her colleagues. She decided to devote all her time to the cause, living on the money she had raised. She would try to keep the suffrage issue at *"fever heat"*, she wrote, and keep the fate of the imprisoned women always in the public eye. She feared that the coming struggle would be long, hard and more intense: and she was right.

The three accused did not deny the charges and the jury found them guilty, although they recommended that their *"undoubtedly pure motives"* should be taken into account and that they should be treated with the utmost leniency. The judge brushed that recommendation aside. He sent the convicted prisoners to jail in the Second Division for seven months.

A battle of wills between the campaigners and the government then followed. Sylvia, in genuine fear for her mother's health, threw herself into a campaign of protest at the heavy sentence. The convicted three threatened hunger strikes. In parliament, the Home Secretary declared: *"Be they leaders or rank and file, forcible feeding will be adopted if they do not take their food."* When Keir Hardie accused him of cruelty, Asquith claimed that any prisoner could walk out of prison that day if they *"would only give an undertaking to refrain from militant action"*.

"You know they cannot!" thundered a Labour MP, leaping to his feet. *"You will go down in history as the man who tortured innocent women! You ought to be driven from public life!"*

Meanwhile, in prison, forcible feeding had begun again. Emmeline Pankhurst was weak from fasting and anxiety but when the doctors and warders appeared in her cell, she resisted them, and was released the following day. Her fellow-accused were not so fortunate: both remained in prison for much longer and both were repeatedly force-fed in that time. During that time, too, the Pethick-Lawrences' house was seized and auctioned by several insurance companies determined to reclaim the money they had had to pay out after the damage caused by the suffragettes' campaign.

▦

Now Asquith finally cast off any last pretence of being neutral on the issue of women's suffrage. In a debate in the House of Commons he dismissed the possibility of women's franchise being included in the Liberals' Franchise Reform Bill as *"an altogether improbable hypothesis"*.

Asquith and his government had taken a tough line, and they were determined to stick to it. Just as governments in the twenty-first century often refuse to negotiate with terrorists until the terrorist acts cease, so Asquith refused to consider the women's suffrage demands unless the suffragette violence was called off.

But his refusal to include women's suffrage in the promised legislation was the spark that set off a fresh blaze of destruction. An extensive campaign of secret – and not so secret – arson attacks was organized, probably under the direction of Christabel from her Paris hideout. (Annie Kenney frequently crossed the Channel to Paris, to discuss strategy with Christabel and carry her instructions back to Britain.)

Young women lugged heavy cans and petrol and paraffin through the night and set fire to untenanted buildings, churches and places of historic interest. On one occasion they tried to burn down the residence of Lewis Harcourt, an anti-suffragist member of Asquith's Cabinet; on another they set fire to a house that was being built for Lloyd George. Mary Leigh and another woman tried to burn down the Theatre Royal in Dublin, where Asquith was due to speak.

Sylvia watched this new policy taking place with grief and regret, her feelings torn. She hated to see historic buildings and works of art attacked, but she admired the heroism and resourcefulness of the militants. And she believed that the government's extraordinary treatment of the suffragettes largely neutralized any harm that the arson campaign might cause to public opinion. But when a message came from Christabel in Paris instructing Sylvia to burn down Nottingham Castle, she flatly refused.

The excitement, drama and danger of civil war was not what Sylvia sought. Instead she now chose to move to the East End of London and concentrate her efforts on rousing working women to the cause. At first her presence there aroused local people to little more than amused curiosity. But when she persisted in her meetings, and when they heard what she had to say, working-class women began to join her organization.

▦

The WSPU suspended all militancy five days before the women's amendments to the Franchise Reform Bill were due to be debated in the House of Commons – but they need not have bothered. A new and unexpected crisis was about to take place. As the debate opened, the Speaker of the House rose to his feet, and dropped a bombshell. His announcement unmasked a problem that even Asquith's government had not predicted. (The government claimed ever afterwards that it had had no part in planning the Speaker's surprise decision.)

The Speaker of the House of Commons is the parliamentary authority on the way in which business takes place. And that day, the Speaker ruled that the amendments could not be made – they were out of order. He declared that if any of the women's suffrage amendments were carried, they would alter the character of the bill so much that it would have to be withdrawn and a new one put forward instead.

No one had predicted such a thing. The MPs were stunned. Even the government was taken aback. At first, Asquith's Cabinet was thankful to have avoided a showdown. But they had a hard job convincing the suffrage organizations that no one in the government had known what the Speaker would say. Unsurprisingly, some accused them of having engineered the whole thing. Asquith said that the Speaker's ruling had not been *"in the least degree anticipated"* by the government, nor by *"the great majority of the House"*. But he knew his government would have a lot of trouble now, and must brace themselves for it.

There was no hope of withdrawing the Franchise Reform Bill and reintroducing it in a form to make amendments possible. The only promise that the government was prepared to make was to allow time in the next session for a private member's bill, if one were introduced.

The next session! A private member's bill! No one could now believe there was a ghost of a chance that women could be enfranchised by a private member's bill. If they accepted that idea they would be back where they had started! And that was somewhere the WSPU leadership were not prepared to go. *"We told you so!"* chanted the speakers at a WSPU rally that evening. *"We told you so! The WSPU has never been wrong!"*

Destructive militancy now broke out on an unparalleled scale as the suffragettes went on a despairing rampage of destruction. They did not seek arrest; in fact many did their best to avoid discovery. And the catalogue of small-scale and large-scale damage was almost endless.

Street lamps were broken in towns all over England. *"Votes for Women"* was painted everywhere. Keyholes were stopped up with lead pellets, cushions of railways carriages slashed, flower beds damaged, and the green turf of golf courses was burned with acid forming the words *"Votes for Women"*. When the royal family went to Balmoral on holiday the King was scandalized to discover that all the flags on his private golf course had been removed, and replaced with ones in purple, white and green – the WSPU colours.

Telephone wires were cut, and fuse boxes destroyed. The Orchid House at Kew Gardens was wrecked, and the Tea Pavilion was burned down. Two country railway stations were burned to the ground. Paintings were hacked with knives in the Manchester Art Gallery, and several London galleries, and grand houses were attacked. Bombs were planted near the Bank of England and other strategic targets. The bombs did not go off, but the act appalled many people, whatever their view on suffrage might have been. The situation seemed to be spinning out of anyone's control.

One woman in Dublin went to the cinema with a handbag filled with gunpowder, which she then tried to light with a match. Another woman in London took over the top deck of an open bus in London and fired stones from a catapult at all the buildings that the bus rumbled past. Those who were arrested faced a "price list" of punishment according to the offences: up to nine months in prison for breaking windows; up to two years for arson.

The WSPU and its leaders were under an enormous strain. Emmeline Pankhurst was in and out of prison, and increasingly frail from hunger strikes. Christabel Pankhurst was still living in Paris to where she had fled the previous year, and although she still tried to run militant activities from there she was inevitably rather out of touch with the members. (She did, however, launch her own newspaper, *The Suffragette*, from exile.) And by now Sylvia was becoming increasingly sidelined in the WSPU by her mother and sister. They both thought her political interests, and particularly her East End activities, were taking her away from the main thrust of WSPU policies.

Sylvia's presence in the East End certainly brought that area of London into the limelight. And her interest in the plight of working women was in line with her father's work in the back streets of Manchester. She also launched her own newspaper, *The Women's Dreadnought*, and her East London Federation of Suffragettes (ELFS) finally broke away from the WSPU and became a separate organization.

The WSPU leadership faltered several times during these bitter months. Emmeline and Christabel dismissed several old and trusted members, such as the Pethick-Lawrences, from the organization. The morale of ordinary members dipped and fund-raising collections dropped. But all the Pankhurst women shared one characteristic: their absolute refusal to allow criticism to deflect them from the course on which they had decided.

Sylvia, joining in the campaign of destruction, was soon arrested. In tears of exhaustion in prison, Sylvia raged in fury that she was serving prison time for breaking a window. She thought it despicable:

> ...that the government had their pound of flesh, that the torture had been going on year after year, that woman after woman had been broken and destroyed, and all because a handful of men stood against us ... and would not give way – some for the sake of their jobs, some for the sake of their pride.

By this time hunger strikes were almost automatic amongst suffragettes, and Sylvia was frightened at the thought of more force-feeding. This time, to try to speed up her release, she added a thirst strike to her hunger strike. After a few days she added a sleep strike as well:

> I began to pace up and down the cell: five steps to the window end, abruptly turning, five steps back to the door; pacing on and on ... I felt very sick and faint, terribly faint, but I would not stop.

Sylvia walked on throughout the night. As the hours passed she stumbled and fell, forced herself back to her feet, and walked on. She walked 28 hours, watched in amazement by the warders who were stunned by her power of endurance. She was released two days later and went straight to a nursing home where she was ordered to bed.

The increased militancy brought condemnation from many quarters, and even some defections from the WSPU. But, whatever people thought about these actions, there is no denying that the campaign brought women into the other suffrage societies in larger numbers than ever, making organizations such as the NUWSS stronger and more powerful.

Some women were disappointed that the suffragettes had not elevated moral standards in public life, in the way in which they had hoped. They watched in dismay as the campaigns made enemies of the very politicians whose support was crucial in the future. Millicent Fawcett was privately acutely distressed at the militant actions, although she would never have condemned them in public.

Asquith

Cat and Mouse

1913

ANTI-SUFFRAGE VIEWS were strengthened by the militant campaigns. The National League for Opposition to Women's Suffrage included such well-known figures as Lord Curzon (the Conservative Party leader in the House of Lords), some prominent women, and members of the royal family. Faced with this volatile situation, the Liberal government needed to step up their response, and curb the militant actions. They had discovered that imprisonment was too often followed by hunger strikes, and even if force-feeding was imposed, prisoners were often released long before their whole sentence was served. The authorities did not want to be outwitted in this way. It was all very well for minor offences like scuffles in the streets or window-breaking; but serious crimes like planting bombs and causing wholesale destruction were another matter.

Lady Bathurst, a leading anti-suffragist, suggested in a letter to the *Morning Post* that the suffragettes should be deported to New Zealand or Australia after being *"birched"* (beaten) and having their heads shaved. Many MPs thought that Asquith's new Home Secretary, Reginald McKenna, was too lenient on the women. But Mr McKenna explained to the House of Commons how difficult it was for the prison authorities to cope with the suffragettes. He detailed how they would refuse to be examined by a doctor, how they surreptitiously starved themselves, and how one of the prisoners had *"sponged herself all over with water"* before going to bed and then had spent the night without any bed clothes, deliberately making herself ill.

Challenged by one MP who said that if the women were left to carry out their threats to die then nothing would happen, Mr McKenna replied:

I think you would find that 30 or 40 would come forward to die. They are fanatical and hysterical women who do not fear death in fighting what they believe to be the cause of women.

But Reginald McKenna knew that somehow, despite these problems, he had to come up with a solution.

By now the country was dizzy with arguments. In the House of Commons there had been bills and amendments to bills, there had been promises made and broken, and parliamentary session after session of talk and argument and failures. But when at last Reginald McKenna introduced a bill that was quickly passed into law as an Act of Parliament, it was not the one for which women hoped, and for which they had fought for years. It was not an Act that would enable women to vote. Instead, it was the Cat and Mouse Act.

The Cat and Mouse Act of 1913 was officially called the Temporary Discharge of Prisoners for Ill-Health Act. But it quickly became known by its other name, and it is easy to see why.

Take one suffragette – the Mouse – and one government official in the shape of a policeman – the Cat. The Mouse is arrested and thrown into a cage by the Cat. But then, in protest, the Mouse refuses to eat. She cannot be allowed to die, of course, for that would make the government look cruel and unreasonable. So the Mouse is forcibly fed. But this force-feeding, this supposed saving of her life, ironically brings her even closer to death than her hunger strike did. So it cannot continue for very long. The cage door will have to be opened, and the Mouse will have to be set free again.

But now, with the Cat and Mouse Act, the story is not over. Now when the Mouse leaves its cage, the Cat follows it. The Cat sits down in front of the Mouse's hole and watches carefully, until it believes that the Mouse is restored to health and so is fit to go back into the cage again. Then the Cat pounces! It carries the Mouse back to the cage and throws it back inside to complete its prison term. Of course, the Mouse will immediately refuse food once more, and once more she will be forcibly fed.

The Mouse must also learn that refusing food in the cage is now an official offence under the rules. Refusing food will also be punished by adding days or even weeks to the original sentence. But the Mouse will soon become ill again, from the hunger strike and from force-feeding. She will have to be let out again to recuperate. Once more the Cat will have a busy time chasing the Mouse around – and so the Mouse will endure weeks or even months of alternating starvation, outrage, illness and recuperation. The idea, of course, was not just to punish the Mouse – but effectively to keep her out of action.

The Cat and Mouse Act was applied with ruthless efficiency and the suffragettes' suffering was intense. The women were released only when their hunger strikes had brought them to the point of extreme weakness and the period of recuperation was kept to a minimum.

A few MPs protested vigorously about the Cat and Mouse Act in parliament. It was courageous of them to do so, for they were isolated and unpopular in such an anti-suffrage House of Commons. Their arguments were booed and mocked, but they persisted. Keir Hardie spoke with particular passion:

Do not torture them in prison and feed them as you would a half-worried rat in a cockpit, and let them out,

*and take them back once more to prison to undergo all
these horrors and tortures.*

But the bill was carried by 296 votes with only 43
against. Fourteen members of the Labour Party voted on
the side of the Liberal government.

Pankhurst

Dying for the Cause

1913

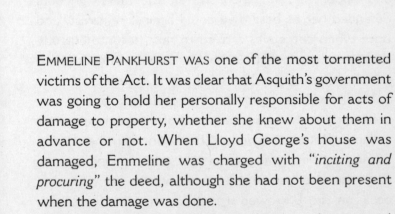

EMMELINE PANKHURST WAS one of the most tormented victims of the Act. It was clear that Asquith's government was going to hold her personally responsible for acts of damage to property, whether she knew about them in advance or not. When Lloyd George's house was damaged, Emmeline was charged with *"inciting and procuring"* the deed, although she had not been present when the damage was done.

Her sentence was shockingly harsh – three years' penal servitude. After nine days without food she was released in an emaciated condition, and then re-arrested after 15 days. Another hunger strike followed, and another release for seven days. And so it went on, month after month. Emmeline was released nine times after hunger and thirst strikes – only to be re-arrested after brief respites.

At one WSPU rally Emmeline was so weak she had to be wheeled on to the platform in an invalid chair. But she never lost her nerve or her courage. *"Even if they kill you and me, victory is assured,"* was her constant message. Sylvia wrote: *"Her sole doubt was that she might die at too small a price"* – in other words, that she might die, and yet votes for women might still not be achieved.

Sylvia went on hunger strike eight times during this period. Always on her release she took refuge in the East End of London where the people had grown to admire and support her, and where she felt safe. Her neighbours defended her as best they could against re-arrest, and once when detectives arrived to take her into custody they were seen off by a hostile crowd of hundreds of people throwing missiles and chanting, *"Cats! Cats!"*

Weak with hunger and thirst strikes, Sylvia was constantly racked with pain and often on the point of collapse. But she carried on her work from her home, writing articles, giving interviews and planning how to elude the detectives and get to her next meeting. On one occasion she borrowed a uniform from her nurse; on another she simply patted rouge on her cheeks and wore a low hat and high-collared coat: Sylvia was known to despise make-up and to hate constricting clothes. Once she reached her destination in a cart wrapped up in a sack and hidden under a pile of wood. Another time her disguise was to carry a fake "baby" stuffed with newspaper. But often she was so weak she had to be carried into meetings in a chair.

"*Sylvia's Army*" was the name given to groups of suffragettes who formed a protective barrier around any of the "mice" who were breaking the terms of their release by speaking in public. They fought with detectives and police who tried to make their arrests, and often won enough time for the "mice" to slip away again. One newspaper ridiculed the army and called the women "*athletic Amazons with broomsticks*" when they appeared in force to guard Sylvia and her supporters. But the tactic worked.

As long as the Cat and Mouse Act was applied to the militant suffragette leaders they could take advantage of the attention and the publicity – and they could court public opinion while they did so. Both Emmeline and Sylvia Pankhurst constantly appeared in public as semi-invalids – the clear victims of Liberal brutality. But it was a very high price to pay.

Later that same year, however, another suffragette showed that she was prepared to pay the highest price of all for the cause. Her name was Emily Wilding Davison.

Emily Davison had been a passionate suffragette for many years. She had long believed in the ideal of personal sacrifice for the cause. Emily was convinced that if one woman deliberately gave her life for women's suffrage, that would create the atmosphere necessary in Britain to win the victory, and finally to bring the sufferings of all the militants to an end. In prison a year earlier, Emily had tried to kill herself three times. Twice she had flung herself over the corridor railings, but both times she had been caught by the wire safety netting 40 feet below (about 12 metres). The third time, she deliberately threw herself down the iron staircase. She survived, but sustained severe injuries from which she never fully recovered.

Emily's determination to die was not encouraged within the suffragette movement. No suffrage organization wanted its members' self-sacrifices to reach this level, and Emily was condemned and ostracized by the WSPU leaders. They saw her as a self-willed person who persisted in acting on her own initiative rather than waiting for, or acting on, official instructions.

It is not clear from Sylvia's account whether or not she shared that judgement of Emily Davison. Sylvia herself was frequently criticized by the WSPU leaders – especially by her mother and sister – so she may well have been sympathetic to someone else who didn't toe the official line. She certainly admired Emily's courage, and talked affectionately of her *"tall, slightly awkward figure, green elusive eyes and ... the small, jauntily poised head"*.

In any event, WSPU disapproval did not deter Emily or deflect her from her course. The day before the Derby race was to be run she laid flowers at the feet of a statue of Joan of Arc, whom many suffragettes regarded as their patron saint – and who had died for the cause she believed in.

The following day, 4 June, Emily travelled with friends to the Derby – the most famous horserace of the year. The group's agreed intention was to protest by standing at Tattenham Corner, on the edge of the racecourse itself, and waving WSPU colours in the air as the horses galloped past. At least, that is what Emily had agreed with her friends, and that is what they thought would happen. But as the horses thundered around the track and headed up towards Tattenham Corner, with thousands of people watching and cheering on their favourites, Emily ducked under the rails, ran out into the race course, and flung herself at a group of racehorses.

It all happened in an instant – and many people who weren't nearby did not realize that anything had gone wrong until the race was over. And it was quite impossible for the jockeys or the horses to take any avoiding action. It was Anmer, a horse that belonged to King George, who knocked Emily to the ground. Her skull was fractured by the impact. She was rushed to a nearby hospital in Epsom and later operated on by a brain surgeon, but her injuries were too great. A week later, Emily Davison died.

No one now knows – any more than Emily's friends did on that day in 1913 – if she changed her mind at the last moment, or if she had always had a secret suicide plan. We do not even know if she really intended to be killed. Many people thought that Emily had deliberately chosen to throw herself under Anmer in a desperate attempt to alert the King to the seriousness of the suffrage cause, and to appeal to him in some way for his support. But it is most unlikely that in the heat of the moment, with horses surging down the track, anyone could have carried out such a plan successfully. It would certainly have been impossible for Emily to pick out the King's colours on the jockey in the midst of all that movement, and then to aim herself at that individual horse. But there is no doubt that Emily's death under Anmer's hooves added an extra layer of significance and drama to the tragedy.

On Saturday 14 June, Emily Davison's body was taken through London from Victoria Station to King's Cross Station with remarkable pageantry and drama. Tens of thousands of women took part in a cavalcade through the streets, marching in carefully co-ordinated and dignified groups. Each of the groups of women was dressed in black, purple or white: those wearing black carried purple irises; those wearing purple carried red peonies; and those wearing white carried laurel wreaths. It was a remarkable sight.

At the head of the procession was a standard-bearer on whose banner was embroidered: "*Thoughts have gone forth whose power can sleep no more. Victory. Victory.*" Then followed groups of hunger strikers – Sylvia Pankhurst walked with them, despite her weakness from a recent prison term – along with many clergymen, personal friends, and members of Emily's family.

Emmeline Pankhurst had planned to attend the funeral, dressed in deep mourning. But as she crossed the pavement outside her house to get into her carriage and travel to Victoria Station she was arrested, to prevent her from attending the funeral and adding to the event's publicity. Before she was taken to Holloway Prison, however, Emmeline left instructions for her empty carriage to follow the hearse all the way to King's Cross, in an almost Victorian mark of respect. From there the coffin was taken north by train, for burial in Emily Davison's home town of Morpeth.

No one watching the procession could fail to be impressed by it. Emily's action was tragic, foolish and misguided – and yet brave enough to be admirable. Sacrificing your life for a cause was something everyone could respond to, even if they didn't agree with the cause. Brave deeds and loud words were one thing; but the waste of a young life was quite another. It was shocking, and it made many people wonder if her death had any point – if it could possibly help achieve anything. Many feared that it could not.

In March 1914 Sylvia put her own health seriously at risk once again. In Holloway Prison she went without food, water and sleep until she was so weary and weak that when she was released on Cat and Mouse licence she was unable to stand without support. But she was already committed to a march on Westminster Abbey and refused to contemplate the idea of letting her supporters down, although her doctors advised her not to go. She was carried to the Abbey on a stretcher by other members of her East London Federation of Suffragettes, most of whom looked almost as ill as Sylvia did because of their own recent imprisonments and hunger strikes.

The spectacle of this famous young woman, frail and thin, being carried through the streets by her supporters who looked far too ill themselves to be walking anywhere, moved many onlookers to compassion and to join the procession. By the time they reached Charing Cross the procession had grown to about 800 people: by the time they reached the Abbey more than 3,000 men and women had joined it.

The Abbey had been locked and barred against the procession, but one defiant priest held a prayer service on the steps. Then Sylvia, exhausted, was taken by ambulance back to the East End. Arrested again the next month, Sylvia returned to Holloway where she again refused food and water, and went without sleep, for a further six days. A letter from her to her mother was printed in the *Daily Chronicle* newspaper:

> I am fighting, fighting, fighting… I have four, five and six wardresses every day as well as the two doctors. I am fed by stomach tube twice a day. I resist all the time.

Despite all this, the Liberal government did not alter its position. But Sylvia then published an open letter to

Asquith in her newspaper, *The Women's Dreadnought*. She stated her intention to return to jail where she would continue a hunger strike – and that even when she was released she would continue the hunger strike until the government agreed to her demands.

> I will not merely hunger strike, but when I am released I will continue my hunger strike at the door of the House of Commons and will not take either food or water until you agree to see my deputation.

Asquith
The Delegation
1914 – 1918

ASQUITH TOOK NO ACTION to rescue Sylvia when she was sent back to prison a few days later. For the moment public opinion was entirely on her side, and all the drama and attention of the women's suffrage movement was entirely focussed on Sylvia, but Asquith remained apparently unmoved, at least in public. In a private letter he wrote:

> *Sylvia Pankhurst, whom McKenna is letting today out of prison – she has been 8 days without food or drink – proposes to continue her 'strike' to the point of suicide. I don't want, if I can help, to secure her the martyr's crown, but que faire? [what can I do?]*

Asquith could not continue to ignore the situation for long: the pressure had become relentless. In May 1914

Sylvia was again out on Cat and Mouse licence from prison, and she organized an East End women's delegation to see the Prime Minister. But at first Asquith refused to receive the delegation.

Sylvia then decided to carry through a desperate plan. When she was re-arrested she would go on a hunger and thirst strike again, and continue that outside prison as well. She said that she would only stop her strike when Asquith agreed to see the deputation. She wrote to the Prime Minister again, laying out her intentions.

Asquith still refused to budge. The situation must have appalled him, but he was determined not to give in to the drama or the emotion of Sylvia's actions.

Sylvia was re-arrested, and started her promised hunger and thirst strike. She was released again on 18 June, and declared herself ready to continue her threat. Friends drove her to the House of Commons, carried her across the road from the car, and put her down on the pavement near the entrance to parliament. A crowd of supporters surrounded her, spilling out into the road. There, she insisted, she would stay – until Asquith received the delegation, or until she died.

It was an extraordinary situation, and no one knew what to do. If the police simply arrested Sylvia she would gain even more sympathy; and if she died there would be a fresh wave of support for her. Asquith must have realized that – even if he hated the idea – he had to concede something.

No one now knows exactly what happened inside the corridors of parliament, but the results were dramatic.

Somehow, Keir Hardie managed to see Asquith in private and talk to him – and somehow, Hardie managed to persuade Asquith to change his mind.

Keir Hardie emerged from the parliament buildings with a message from the Prime Minister, and gave it to Sylvia and her supporters. Asquith had relented! He would see a delegation of six women the following day. The women crowded around Sylvia, laughing and cheering. *"We are winning! At last we are winning!"*

The six East End women on the next day's delegation made the utmost of their opportunity. They poured out the details of the harshness of their lives and their low wages to the Prime Minister. One of them, a brush-maker, slapped down a brush she had made, and for which she had been paid a penny-farthing, in front of him. (A penny-farthing in old money would be worth about 5p in today's decimal currency.) She declared: *"I do all the work! I keep my home! I ought to have the vote for it!"* Unanimously they pressed their demand – the vote for every woman over 21.

The Prime Minister listened carefully to what the women had to say, and he seemed impressed by their comments on women's working conditions. He entirely agreed with them that, if women were to be given the vote, they must be given it on the same terms as men. He made great play of the point that, if a change was to come, then *"it must be democratic in its basis"*. But he still made no pledge that his government would take any action.

The women were convinced that his interest was genuine and that his attitude was softening. That may have been the case. Asquith was genuinely interested in working conditions, and factory health and safety. One of the first pieces of legislation he had developed as a young politician in the 1890s had been a Factories and Workshops Act, intended to tighten up health and safety rules.

He may even have seen that the women's arguments could offer him a way to produce a solution to the difficulties, and yet still save his own and his government's face. It is perfectly possible that – in his wily political fashion – he was preparing the ground for a change of position.

We will never know now if that was true or not. Eight weeks later, an all-consuming distraction intervened. The country was at war with Germany: the First World War had been declared.

The war created an urgent need to reform the voting laws. Millions of men who were away from home fighting lost their qualification to vote because of that. The old laws required voters to live in their place of residence for 15 months before an election. So if members of the armed forces were going to be able to vote whilst they were away from home, the government was clearly going to have to revise the law. That put the issue of women's suffrage back on the table again, and the government ordered the preparation of a parliamentary report on the whole suffrage subject.

In August 1916, after two years of war, the government revived the suffrage debate. Asquith shocked the House of Commons as well as the rest of the country by declaring that if the franchise was to be extended – well then, British women had an *"unanswerable"* case for being included. He continued:

> *During this war, the women of this country have rendered as effective service ... as any other class of the community ... When the war comes to an end have not the women a special claim to be heard on the many questions which will arise directly affecting their interests?*

And Asquith finished his speech with an extraordinary statement that effectively marked the end of his public opposition to women's suffrage. *"I say quite frankly,"* he announced, *"that I cannot deny their claim."*

Pankhurst
Equal Votes at Last
1914 – 1918

THE OUTBREAK OF WAR split the suffrage movement. Sylvia and many other suffragettes opposed the war, but whatever their views were, none of the suffrage organizations wanted to continue their protests or militant actions while Britain was at war with a foreign state. Conscription came into effect almost at once, which meant that all young men in reasonable health were called up to serve in the British armed forces. Christabel returned from Paris, and she and her mother threw themselves enthusiastically into the call-up activities. They handed out white feathers (representing cowardice) to young men who were not in uniform, and called for enemy aliens who lived in the country to be interned (imprisoned).

Sylvia wept with despair at her mother's support of the recruitment campaign: she thought it was a tragic betrayal of their movement. She remained a firm advocate for peace, spoke at anti-conscription rallies, and never supported the war efforts. But she did not support any militant action during this period.

Conscription had one positive effect for women: it made their war work essential. Women took over the work that men had done in industries, transport and other services, and showed they were perfectly capable of doing it. But for Sylvia's women in the East End, the war brought additional suffering. Prices of ordinary food and other essential goods shot up, while some factories also closed down bringing unemployment and extra hardship.

When Asquith made his speech announcing the end to his opposition to women's suffrage, its supporters held their breath in disbelief. It seemed unbelievable, but it appeared to be true — the old enemies had been converted and whilst they had not exactly become friends, at least they were no longer in unwavering opposition. Was it all too good to be true? Sylvia thought not; she even wrote to Asquith congratulating him on what he had said, which probably annoyed him. Even *Punch*, a satirical magazine, published a cartoon of a woman conductor welcoming Asquith on to her bus with the words, *"Better late than never."*

Times had changed, it seemed, and people's minds had changed with the times. Not everyone was converted: Lord Curzon and Mrs Humphrey Ward stood firm in their opposition. But many of their anti-suffrage followers had melted away – the women who had supported them were now openly expressing a change of opinion, and men were also deserting the anti-suffrage cause in large numbers.

There were now many reasons for giving women the franchise. It was not only the fear that, if women did not get the vote, they would resume their militant actions as soon as the war was over, or the general feeling that women had "earned" the vote through their work during the war years. In 1917 there was a revolution in Russia, and a fear that similar violence could engulf Britain was in the air. An extension of voting rights – to more men as well as to at least some women – was considered one way to avoid similar social unrest.

But before the parliamentary report that Asquith had ordered was made public, Asquith's Cabinet had lost control of the wartime coalition government. David Lloyd George became Prime Minister instead of Asquith. This in turn split the Liberal Party, and Asquith's group of Liberals lost political power forever. It was a bitter blow for him, but perhaps Asquith was also relieved that he did not have to preside over the final days of male-only suffrage.

In 1917 a House of Commons bill recommended votes for all men over 21, and for women over 30 who were university graduates, as well as women who were house owners or tenant householders (or the wives of either).

(The qualifying age for women was raised to 30 as consolation for the remaining anti-suffrage groups, and the bill was put forward from the House of Commons rather than from the government. That saved Asquith's face as well as those of his anti-suffrage friends.) Sylvia attacked the blatant discrimination of the limited women's suffrage terms but to her disgust all the other suffrage groups, including the WSPU, accepted it meekly.

The suffragettes' acceptance of the limited bill may have seemed meek, but the women were not prepared to leave the passage through parliament of even this compromise, to chance. A big demonstration – the first during the war – was organized in the form of a women war-workers march. Representatives from 70 different trades, ranging from lamplighters and engine cleaners to the more usual nurses, teachers and lace-makers, took to the streets of London and then to a speakers' platform to reiterate their support for women's suffrage.

A similar deputation gathered to see the new Prime Minister, Lloyd George, a month later. Every member of the new Cabinet was also visited. The women had not forgotten how to organize and demonstrate.

On 19 June 1917 the Ladies' Gallery at the House of Commons was filled to capacity. Many of the women who attended that day had done so many times in the past, only to hear their cause mocked, obstructed, deliberately neglected and outvoted. Now they gathered to hear the final debate, and watch the MPs vote on the new legislation.

"The fight is out of the whole struggle," said one MP. *"It is absolutely clear that the fight is won."* Even so, the vote was larger than anyone had expected. Three hundred and eighty-five MPs voted in favour of women's suffrage, while only 55 voted against it. It was victory – a limited victory, certainly, but a real one at last.

Suffragists had always been afraid that the House of Lords might yet block any favourable legislation. Asquith's government had limited the power of the Lords, but it was still possible that their expected opposition could damage the Representation of the People Bill, perhaps by forcing amendments to it. The Lords could also further delay the bill if they wanted to, and who knew what yet more delays would mean? The House of Lords were not as susceptible to pressure as MPs were, for they were not elected. They had no voters to send them deputations or telegrams, or threaten to withdrawal support.

And the House of Lords had always been a stronghold of opposition to women's suffrage. Lord Curzon was still President of the Anti-Suffrage League, and he was the leader of the House of Lords. There were plenty of others whose opposition was known to be both strong, and influential, and they would vote with Curzon. Would the opposition carry the day? There was little the women could do except worry, and wait.

In the event, the whole bill passed smoothly through the House of Lords, just as in the House of Commons. There were certainly speeches against it, and many of the old arguments were trotted out – but, as in the Commons, many speeches also reflected a new mood of acceptance and understanding.

When Lord Curzon rose to speak at last, it was to say that the passage of the Representation of the People Bill would be the ruin of the country. Women were politically worthless, he believed, and the whole ideal of women's suffrage and the women's movement was disastrous and wrong. But, he added, it was too late to oppose it now. If the Lords voted against the bill, why then the House of Commons would simply send it back to them again. He could not, and did not, recommend that destructive course to the Lords.

The Lords' vote was taken. One hundred and thirty-four of them voted in favour of the bill, with only 71 against it.

So the Representation of the People Bill was through both Houses! On 6 February 1918 it received the Royal Assent and became the law of the land.

At the beginning of 1918 almost eight and a half million women were entitled to vote for the first time (as well as almost 13 million men, now that men could vote from the age of 21). Fifty years of struggle was over – for it had been 50 years since the first Women's Suffrage Bill had been introduced to the House of Commons.

National elections were called at the end of the war, later that year. The Prime Minister declared that women not only had the right to vote, but could also stand for parliamentary election. A bill to enable women to stand for election to the House of Commons was hurried through both Houses of Parliament, in time for the general election in December 1918.

Sixteen women did stand for election, including Christabel Pankhurst, but only one was elected (and that one, a Sinn Fein leader, would not swear the oath of allegiance and so did not take up her seat). Then one year later Nancy Astor won a parliamentary seat in a by-election, after her husband joined the House of Lords, so she was the first woman Member of Parliament. Lady Astor was rich, married to an aristocrat and American-born – so her success was probably rather annoying for the suffragettes who had fought for so long to get the vote. Worse still, Lady Astor had never been a suffragette nor even been interested in women's suffrage. It must have seemed rather an anticlimax.

▦

Women were a political novelty in the years immediately after the First World War. No one had had to take their views into account before, and no political party knew the best way to do that. But letters from female constituents were no longer thrown in the waste-paper basket – they received proper replies, the representatives of women's organizations were now welcomed at Westminster, and the House of Commons was opened once more to women visitors.

Some politicians had feared that women would vote in a solid block, as women, and might seek to form a

Women's Party. In fact Christabel Pankhurst had drawn up a manifesto for a Women's Party in 1917, but it never got further than talk. Most British women saw the vote as a means to an end – as a way of securing reforms, just as Sylvia Pankhurst had said years before when she pointed out that women wanted the vote for the same reasons as men: to achieve change through the ballot box. At last women could begin to work towards that.

Now that women had achieved the vote – or at least now that some of them had – the main protagonists of the WSPU fight moved on to other things. Both Emmeline and Christabel had lectured in the United States to rally support for the war effort. With the war over and with their own battle won, both of them drifted away from politics for a time. Christabel, who was later made a Dame of the British Empire, became deeply religious and lectured on the Second Coming of Christ. Emmeline opened a teashop in the south of France, but in 1928 she returned to Britain to stand as a Conservative candidate in the East End of London – Sylvia's political stronghold.

Sylvia was dismayed at her mother's betrayal – of Richard Pankhurst's radical memory, of Emmeline's previous support for socialism and the Labour Party, and of Sylvia's own work. But Emmeline did not live to fight the election. The jaundice she had developed as a result of her hunger strikes returned, and she now lacked the strength to resist it. She died in June 1928, one month before her 70th birthday.

In the same year, and almost without effort, the last political restrictions on women were swept away. A Further Representation of the People Act gave the vote to all women over the age of 21 – about another five million women. (The voting age in Britain was not lowered to 18 until 1969.) The Prime Minister of the time, Stanley Baldwin, told the House of Commons that it would never again be possible to blame parliament for *"any position of inequality"*. He added, *"women will have, with us, equal rights. The justification for the old agitation is gone, and gone for ever."*

Millicent Fawcett was present in the visitors' gallery of the House of Lords, in 1928, to hear that Act pass its final reading. She wrote later of the experience:

> *It is almost 61 years since I heard John Stuart Mill introduce his suffrage amendment to the Reform Bill on May 20th 1867. So I have had the extraordinary good luck in having seen the struggle from the beginning.*

This was a victory for three generations of women who had fought for the vote using just about every tactic possible – from genteel and well-mannered persuasion to the most violent and militant confrontations.

Keir Hardie's death in September 1915 – the loss of her *"truest of friends"* – had hit Sylvia hard, but grief did not slow her down for long. And, unlike her mother and sister, Sylvia did never seen the right to vote as an end in itself, so she found it easy to direct her energies to other social issues. She was soon caught up in the revolutionary ideals that shook the post-war world. Her East London Federation of Suffragettes was renamed the Workers' Socialist Federation, and Sylvia threw herself into support for the revolution in Russia. In 1920 her noisy political opposition to the British government brought her one final prison sentence, for sedition (encouraging people to rebel against their government). She was still so ill from her previous experiences that she spent the whole six months in the prison hospital.

Sylvia did not choose to stand for parliament, although she was invited to do so several times. By now she believed that the British parliamentary system was corrupt and beyond reform. In 1928, when the Further Representation of the People Act was passed, Sylvia did not celebrate the day. By then she was living happily in the English countryside with an Italian revolutionary called Silvio Corio and their baby son. Sylvia refused to marry her lover, and her son was named Richard Keir Pethick Pankhurst – Richard for her father; Keir for Keir Hardie; and Pethick for the Pethick-Lawrences from Sylvia's WSPU days. Being an unmarried mother was still thought scandalous, and her choosing to become one at the age of 42 raised many eyebrows. Even her mother and sister disapproved of Sylvia's decision. But disapproval had never stopped Sylvia from doing what she thought was right.

Earl of Oxford and Asquith

Asquith

1916 – 1928

AT THE BEGINNING OF the First World War Asquith had been the Prime Minister of Britain for six years. But two years after the war began he was defeated as the Liberal leader. Instead David Lloyd George became both the leader of the party and Prime Minister.

Asquith's friends and colleagues were dismayed at their leader's defeat. Together with Asquith they refused to serve in Lloyd George's government, but their protest had little effect, and Asquith refused to attack Lloyd George or indulge in political in-fighting as long as the war continued. By the time it ended Lloyd George was seen as the man who had won the war for Britain, while Asquith and his friends were criticized. In East Fife, during the 1918 election campaign, Asquith was greeted by a poster that read: *"Asquith nearly lost you the War. Are you going to let him spoil the Peace?"* Like many of his

149

former Liberal Party Cabinet members, Asquith lost his parliamentary seat in that election, and the Liberal Party that had dominated British politics for more than 70 years was in ruins.

Asquith had endured many public difficulties and setbacks in his parliamentary years; the war and added personal tragedies with the death in battle of one of his sons and the serious injury of another. But Asquith's usual response to difficulties was to throw himself deeper into work, and that is exactly what he did in the post-war years. He never gave up politics. In 1920, during yet another election campaign (this time in Paisley), he wrote this to a friend, making it clear that he had not changed his mind about votes for women:

There are about 15,000 women on the [electoral] register here. They are a dim, impenetrable, for the most part ungettable element – of whom all that one knows is that they are for the most part hopelessly ignorant of politics, credulous to the last degree, and flickering with gusts of sentiment like a candle in the wind.

Asquith later returned to the House of Commons and to the Liberal Party leadership, but he never held government office again. In 1923 King George V gave Asquith a title – the Earl of Oxford and Asquith – and after that he could take a seat in the House of Lords. He died on 15 February 1928.

Pankhurst

The End of the Story

1928 – 1960

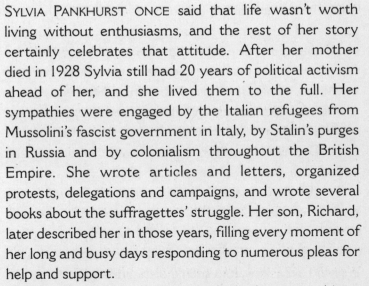

SYLVIA PANKHURST ONCE said that life wasn't worth living without enthusiasms, and the rest of her story certainly celebrates that attitude. After her mother died in 1928 Sylvia still had 20 years of political activism ahead of her, and she lived them to the full. Her sympathies were engaged by the Italian refugees from Mussolini's fascist government in Italy, by Stalin's purges in Russia and by colonialism throughout the British Empire. She wrote articles and letters, organized protests, delegations and campaigns, and wrote several books about the suffragettes' struggle. Her son, Richard, later described her in those years, filling every moment of her long and busy days responding to numerous pleas for help and support.

Christabel and Sylvia had had many bitter disagreements over many years and they never

151

reconciled or worked together again. The only time the two sisters met during the 44 years between the end of the First World War and Christabel's death in the United States in 1958, was at their mother's funeral. (Adela, the youngest Pankhurst sister, had moved to Australia in 1914. She was one of the founders of the Australian Communist Party, and died in 1961.)

Sylvia's connections with Italy led to the last great enthusiasm of her life – the African country of Ethiopia, then called Abyssinia. When Mussolini invaded Abyssinia in 1935 Sylvia Pankhurst rallied support for Abyssinia and its Emperor, Haile Selassie. (When they finally met, Sylvia briskly told Haile Selassie that she was a republican and didn't approve of emperors – but she supported him against Mussolini's aggression because his cause was a just one.) After the Second World War she flung herself into battle to free the former Italian colonies in Africa, which included Abyssinia. She visited the country several times and raised funds for a modern hospital in the capital of Addis Ababa. When her partner Silvio Corio died in 1950, Sylvia moved to Addis Ababa to live. She died on 27 September 1960.

The Emperor Haile Selassie attended her magnificent funeral in the cathedral in Addis Ababa, and she was buried in the plot set aside for Ethiopian patriots. It is rather ironic that Sylvia, who had never been interested in grand occasions, had such a distinguished burial.

Afterword

IN 1914, NOT A SINGLE woman was allowed to vote at a parliamentary election in Britain. Four years later women over 30 could vote; by 1928 all women over 21 could vote – the same age qualification as for men. When John Stuart Mill proposed in 1866 that women should be granted the parliamentary vote some MPs had laughed out loud, they thought the idea so ludicrous. In 1928 the laughter came from victorious women.

The cause of women's suffrage seemed agonizingly slow to its supporters. The years of frustration and confusion were very hard to bear. But the twentieth-century campaign developed at an extraordinary speed from discussions in drawing rooms and at tea parties into brawls between women and policemen in Parliament Square. But militancy tapped into dangerous sources of deep and previously concealed resentments on both sides. Over 1,000 suffragettes were imprisoned for demanding that women should have the right to vote.

The fight for suffrage encouraged the growing participation of women, not just in politics, but also in demanding much greater opportunities at school and work, and in individual freedom. The struggle for women's suffrage – when thousands of women from very different social backgrounds joined together in a common cause – was fought alongside other campaigns: such as the fight to change the divorce laws, so that women had more control of their earnings and property, and campaigns to open up higher education and the professions to women.

The Pankhurst women were a potent symbol of a new and ultimately irresistible force. They showed what can happen when a significant group of protesters withdraws their consent from the government of the day.

Many historians believe that the WSPU campaign played a major part in women obtaining the vote. Others argue that women's suffrage would have come about more quickly without the actions of the WSPU – that militant actions and violence slowed down the process. Many politicians at the time claimed the same thing. No one now can tell for sure what would have happened without that direct action – without the campaign that the Pankhursts led. Certainly, nothing much had happened *before* they began it. But it is true that by 1914 the conflict had swung into a vicious cycle of action and counter actions that was hard to break. It is difficult to see how the problems would have been resolved, if the First World War had not put the battle on hold. The pattern of misunderstandings between the MPs in the House of Commons on one side, and the suffragette movement outside parliament on the other, ran deep. Neither side truly understood how the other functioned.

Herbert Gladstone, who was Asquith's Home Secretary in 1909, wrote later to a member of the NUWSS to explain what went wrong:

> *The fatal mistake made by the militants was to think that they can cut short the necessary propaganda work by menacing and annoying Cabinet Ministers.*

Gladstone acknowledged that women, through no fault of their own, had an *"imperfect understanding"* of how politics worked because they were denied the vote, but he continued:

> *The fact remains that our [parliamentary] machinery is not adapted for the immediate and successful treatment of questions on which parties are divided.*

Perhaps, if the whole suffrage movement had been more single-minded in their approach, then success might have come faster and with less anger and anguish. Perhaps, if MPs had better explained the political process to outsiders, they would have attracted less suspicion and resentment. But "perhaps" is another world.

Although they were enemies on opposite sides in a bitter and often violent battle, Henry Asquith and Sylvia Pankhurst had more in common than either of them probably realized, or than either would have wanted to acknowledge. Both of them were stubborn people. Both were utterly determined, even ruthless, once they had set their minds to something: all their energies were directed at the goal. Asquith's *"Sledgehammer"* nickname tells us a lot about his style, and Sylvia was famous for her passionate commitment to the cause. They both inspired great devotion in their followers and admirers, as well as great enmity from those who opposed them. No one who knew either Sylvia or Asquith ever remained neutral about them.

Asquith did not think women's suffrage ought to be a major issue for the Liberal Party. He judged that it was politically safe to ignore the suffragettes' demands, and concentrate on other issues instead – pension reforms, Home Rule for Ireland, and restructuring the House of Lords, for example. By the time he had been proved wrong in his judgements about women's suffrage the tide of opinion and events had swept past him – and then he could no longer control or influence the results as he wished. But he never admitted that he had been wrong. He probably never thought he had been.

Further Reading

Dare to be Free: a Women's History Resource Pack by Jean Holder and Katharine Milcoy (Fawcett Library, London Guildhall University, 1997)

Sylvia and Christabel Pankhurst by Barbara Castle (Penguin, 1987)

Shoulder to Shoulder: a Documentary by Midge MacKenzie (Penguin, 1975)

The Asquiths by Colin Clifford (John Murray, 2002)

Votes for Women by Roger Fulford (Faber, 1957)

Asquith by Roy Jenkins (Collins, 1964)

Suffragists and Liberals by David Morgan (Blackwell, 1975)

The Suffragette Movement by Sylvia Pankhurst (Longman, 1931, reprinted by Virago with a foreword by her son, Richard Pankhurst)

E. Sylvia Pankhurst by Patricia W. Romero (Yale University Press, 1987)

The Cause by Ray Strachey (Bell & Sons, 1928)

Acknowledgements

Picture insert
1 Herbert Asquith, 1908 © Topham Picturepoint
2 Asquith cartoon © Mary Evans Picture Library/The Women's Library
3 Two suffragettes with Asquith © Museum of London/HIP
4 Sylvia Pankhurst speaking in the East End © Topham Picturepoint
5 Leading suffragettes © Mary Evans Picture Library
6 Emmeline Pankhurst © Museum of London/HIP
7 Prisoner's Brooch © Mary Evans Picture Library/The Women's Library
8 Force-feeding poster © Museum of London/HIP
9 Cat and Mouse Act poster © Topham Picturepoint
10 Sylvia speaks © Hulton Archive/Getty Images

Index